ICELANDIC JOURNAL

ICELANDIC JOURNAL

BY
ALICE SELBY

EDITED BY
A. R. TAYLOR

VIKING SOCIETY FOR NORTHERN RESEARCH
UNIVERSITY COLLEGE LONDON
1974

Made and printed in Great Britain
by Titus Wilson and Son Ltd., Kendal

© 1974 Viking Society for Northern Research

This work is published simultaneously as *Icelandic Journal* by Alice Selby, edited by A. R. Taylor (Viking Society for Northern Research, University College London, 1974) and as *Saga-Book of the Viking Society for Northern Research* XIX 1 (1974).

PREFACE

TO ONE who in 1933 made a similar journey and who has always regretted the loss of his own diary from that time, it has given some pleasure to prepare the manuscript of Miss Alice Selby's journal for publication. I have tried to identify some of the people she met, but I am afraid a few of the identifications remain conjectural. Unfortunately I was unable to go to Iceland this summer and I have relied on works of reference and on enquiries made by letter. I wish here to record my sincere gratitude for information received from Mr Klemenz Tryggvason of the Hagstofa in Reykjavík, from Mr Bjarni Vilhjálmsson of the Þjóðskjalasafn, from Mr Steindór Steindórsson of Akureyri, and above all from my friend, Mr Eiríkur Benedikz, of the Icelandic Embassy in London. If there are mistakes they must not be blamed: the responsibility is mine.

I have not aimed at absolute consistency in the spelling of Icelandic place-names and personal names in the journal itself. The only Icelandic diacritic retained is the acute accent and that normally only over the letter "a" and in a few names seldom met with. In the notes and in any Icelandic word quoted in the text the appropriate Old or Modern Icelandic spelling has been retained.

Miss Dorothea Selby, sister of the author, brought the journal to the notice of Professor Kenneth Cameron of Nottingham University and President of the Viking Society, and he recommended it to the Society's Council and Editors. Miss Dorothea Selby made publication possible by a generous donation, and she also prevailed on Mr Hibbard to contribute his "personal recollection" of Miss Alice Selby, found at the end of the book. The journal now appears both as an independent publication and as a part of the *Saga-Book*, and I feel sure that many readers will be delighted by Miss Selby's human and often amusing account of her experiences.

A. R. TAYLOR

CONTENTS

1 REYKJAVIK AND THE LAND OF DREAMS .. 7
2 AKUREYRI AND EYJAFJORD 22
3 AKUREYRI AGAIN AND A JOURNEY TO THE EAST 38
4 A RIDE IN SKAGAFJORD 76
5 RETURN TO REYKJAVIK AND FAREWELL .. 87

ALICE SELBY. A PERSONAL RECOLLECTION BY G. R. HIBBARD 94

Chapter One

REYKJAVIK AND THE LAND OF DREAMS

I LEFT Hull on the "Godafoss" on June 19th, 1931. The boat seemed small and uncomfortable. There were twelve passengers in the first class, four English, four German and four Icelandic.

The first few days were blank. The weather was grey and cold, and the sea restless. Till we passed the Pentland Firth I was still more or less alive and conscious of the bleak grey lands and the bleak grey sea. Then for the next two days my world was bounded by a rather unsteady cabin wall with a few dresses rocking uneasily on the cabin pegs. It was not until the afternoon of the third day that my horizon extended itself and I crept up into the pale clear sunshine of the deck. It was cheering to know that we should get our first far-off glimpse of Iceland in the evening, and on the strength of that prospect I had roast pork for dinner and was even able to feel romantic when, far off in the north, in the rose glow of the sunset, we saw an incandescent point and were told that it was Eyjafjallajokul. The air is so clear that the glacier snows can be seen for sixty miles.

At seven in the morning I came on deck to what the picture captions used to call "a land of dreams come true". A huge cliff fell precipitously from a green velvet head to a milky sea at the foot. The dark rocks where the seabirds congregated and left their mark were streaked with white. Gulls were screaming and plunging round the boat. The little town of Vestmannaeyjar lay at the foot of a volcanic mountain, while away in the distance to the left the glaciers of Iceland, Eyjafjallajokul and Hekla (which strictly speaking is not a glacier but at that time was indistinguishable from the genuine jokuls because the snows were lying on the summit), were glittering in the early morning sunshine. I went below, dressed, and then went ashore in a motor-boat from which women in the pretty little Icelandic berets were climbing on board the "Godafoss".

The Vestmannaeyjar are a group of some fourteen islands, though only one of these, Heimaey, is of any importance. The geological composition is different from that of Iceland, and the crags and black cliffs that surround the harbour are more spectacular and theatrically picturesque than anything I was to see in Iceland. The islands have a tragic history of rapine and disease. Lock-jaw was so prevalent at one time that very few of the new-born children survived. It was not until 1847 that Dr Schleisner discovered a prophylactic, the so-called 'navel-oil', and the scourge was removed.[1] The ravages of pirates are memorised in the little headland Ræningjatangi, Robbers' Point, where in the seventeenth century the 'Turks' landed from three Algerian pirate ships, burned, killed and looted, and carried off a large number of the inhabitants into slavery. Some of them were released a few years later, but it was only a handful who found their way back from distant Africa to these northern islands. One of the refugees was the priest of the parish who left a description of the tragic event.[2] For many years afterwards watch against the 'Turks' was kept on the headland, and the houses were protected by a dike or embankment of earth.

The once unhappy little island is now a flourishing port, and the boats call at least once a week. On shore I had my first sight of what is one of the most characteristic sights in the Icelandic towns, the cod-fish drying. This

[1] See K. Kålund, *Bidrag til en historisk-topografisk Beskrivelse af Island* (1877–82), I 282 and footnote.
[2] The raid took place in 1627. There were two priests in Vestmannaeyjar at this time, (a) Jón Þorsteinsson who was killed by the raiders and (b) Ólafur Egilsson who was carried off but released in the following year. He left an account of the incident which has been printed more than once, see *Tyrkjaránið á Íslandi* (ed. Jón Þorkelsson, Sögurit IV, 1906–9).

fish, which is exported in large quantities, mainly for the Friday fare of the Spanish, is washed, split and gutted, and then set in the sun to dry. Every morning the fish is packed on wooden litters, which are then carried by two people to the drying ground. The fish is then unpacked and spread out; it lies there in the sun till evening, when it is again packed on the litter and carried to the tarpaulin-covered stack. Women, girls and little boys carry out this work. It is a pretty scene, with the white fish bleaching like linen in the sun, and the girls in their blue dungarees, and the women with white kerchiefs. Later, when I reached Reykjavik, I found the arrangements for drying fish were more elaborate and included even a miniature railway — the only one in Iceland. I am bound to say that I was never fortunate enough to see the railway function; but I walked along the rusty lines which ran through a desert of dry, shining fish-scales that crackled under the feet like sand above high-water mark, and which didn't smell as disagreeable as one might expect.

As it was still early morning when I stepped ashore at Vestmannaeyjar I did not see the town in its gayest aspect. Except for the girls carrying out the fish, and the little crowd of people on the quay, the inhabitants were all asleep. The town is not impressive. There are many one-story houses of wood and corrugated iron, most of them painted grey or white. Towards the edge of the town there are larger houses, villas of concrete, each standing in a little patch of grass, railed off from the un-made road with wire fencing. There were several motor lorries, a café, a picture-house and a barber's shop with a collection of depressing bead necklaces.

The hooting of the steamer called me from an examination of the barber's window, and we were soon off again. The day was bright but so cold. To starboard we had the jokuls glittering in the sun, and after that only a long line of intimidating coast with sands and barren lava fields. Then, far far away in the distance, the white mass of Snæfellsjokul rose out of the sea, sixty miles away.

We rounded Reykjanes, and the sun went in. Reykjavik was a desolate little grey cluster as we neared it over the grey and choppy sea. And when I landed the feeling of greyness persisted. Grey buildings of corrugated iron and bigger, newer ones of concrete. Grey streets lead to a grey lake, and a grey sun occasionally peers through the grey clouds.

But one bit of colour caught my eye. I had hoped, but not expected, to find gaily dressed Vikings striding the streets of Reykjavik. So when I looked round at the clatter of hoofs and saw a romantic figure on a horse, I felt that I was back in the Saga Age. The man was gold-helmeted and scarlet cloaked. He had a red beard, and his blue trousers were laced with gold thongs. He had a gold spear in his hand and a dog at his side.[3] It was later that I learned how the Viking got his outfit. There is a movement for restoring the national costume, but this ideal gets no more sympathy from the majority of people in Reykjavik than does the Dress Reform Movement from most Londoners. So, as a protest against this freak ideal, some bright young people clubbed together and bought a complete Viking outfit. They gave this to a harmless lunatic who hangs about the town and flaunts his finery to the surprise and delight of foreigners.

Apart from this touch of medievalism, Reykjavik is no more romantic than any other town. There is a very fine hotel with a ball-room and innumerable bathrooms with hot and cold. This hotel, I was told, was built by an ex-champion of *glíma* (a form of wrestling which is the national and traditional sport in Iceland).[4] This man made a fortune in exhibiting the art at music-halls and

---

[3] Oddur Sigurgeirsson. For a photograph of this well-known figure see W. H. Auden and Louis Macneice, *Letters from Iceland* (1937), 219.

[4] Jóhannes Jósefsson (1883–1968).

circuses all over Europe and returned to his native land to invest the fortune in a fine hotel. There are other hotels, comfortable if not so pretentious. There are two picture theatres, and there is a scheme for building a proper theatre, to be financed by the money gained in taxes from the more popular, if less dignified sister art, the cinema. The shops, though they seem a little dowdy to one used to Bond Street, are not entirely contemptible. I was shocked when I arrived at the absence of what I should describe as "a proper book-shop", but during my six weeks absence in the country a very fine book-shop was opened with national and international literature in plenty.[5]

I had been met at the boat by kind friends, who set out with me on a Grand Tour of Reykjavik, not a lengthy business, for the whole town can be surrounded in half an hour's walk. We saw the Post Office, the Banks, the House of Parliament, the Museum-cum-library, the School, the lake, and the suburbs with their rather dashing new houses. I was shown examples of the flora of Iceland (till then I had hardly been aware that there was one), and I felt patronising at the rather wind-blown tulips and the stunted aquilegia. When I came back to Reykjavik I found the town a-flower with lupins, poppies and even delphiniums. There was also a fine display of red currants, but when I first arrived in late June the flowering season had hardly started. The rhubarb, however, was being harvested. After the allotments we worked back into the town, passing the very modern building where the sculptor Einar Jonsson[6] and his works are housed. In the course of our walk we met most of the passengers and staff from the "Godafoss" and also the only Icelander I had met before starting to Iceland, a girl whom I knew in Copenhagen. I began to perceive dimly a fact, that was later born out in full, that

[5] Briem's bookshop was opened on 1 August 1931. Miss Selby's implied criticism of the two already existing bookshops of Snæbjörn Jónsson and Sigfús Eymundsson seems scarcely justified.
[6] Einar Jónsson (1874–1954).

it is impossible to avoid anyone in Iceland. My journeyings became an absurd picaresque where people I had met in the North or East appeared in an apparently unmotivated way in the South or West. This caused me surprise at first, but I had hardly realised (a) that the inhabitants of Iceland only number 100,000 altogether and (b) that the inhabited area of the country is surprisingly small to the mind of one who is used to the tightly packed districts of Southern and Midland England.

The wind was cold, so we spent what was left of the evening in the pictures. When we came out at 11.30 there was no dark, but only a cold grey corpse-light. I spent the night on the boat.

No meals are served while in port, so next morning I crept out to find some breakfast. It was coffee and slices of sweet cake. After the first morning I benefited by the insistence of two of my companions who managed, though they spoke no Icelandic, to squeeze some quite convincing bread-and-butter from the girl in the café.

I paid a call on a lady to whom I had an introduction, and she, coming in from the garden with her hands stained from rhubarb-picking, received me with the courtesy and self-possession which I was to find characteristic of the Icelander confronted by a stranger, and further a stranger with but little knowledge of their language. I was whisked off in a car to see the famous hot springs and hot houses about ten miles from Reykjavik. We humped over a rough road through bleak stretches of lava country. A rough road, I say, but when I returned to Reykjavik from the country, I realised that this particular road is one of the finest in the country and is smooth as glass in comparison with many parts of the long main road that joins the North and South. The first enquiry of the solicitous when one steps into a car is "Do you get *bílveikur?*", i.e. car-sick. It is the most ordinary thing in Iceland to stop the touring cars to allow a passenger to indulge the weaknesses of the flesh. There are two or perhaps three causes for the frequency of this distressing ailment. One is the actual surface of the road, and here a further discomfort may arise — that is the danger of hitting your head on a beam in the roof of the car when it leaps, and the passengers with it, at some particularly large bump in the road. The second cause is the direction of the roads, many of which, as far as I could make out, are simply a widening of the little twisting pony tracks. When these were enlarged for cars it didn't seem to strike the engineers that the curves might profitably have been shaved off. Thirdly, I think that the Icelander's car-sickness is due to lack of practice in riding in motor-cars. It is still a novelty to a great many of them. Indeed, many young people's only idea of a binge is to hire a car and drive it anywhere, preferably with a convivial party and several bottles.

The lava country is desolate with nothing but grass and rocks. I asked if it was capable of being cultivated, and my friend replied that cultivation was possible but the difficulty was shortage of labour. The people in Iceland are so few. In the holidays all the young people, men, boys and girls, try to get some sort of work — very often road-making. It is considered the manly thing to do, so even rich boys work. This year, however, unemployment is much commoner than it was because of the world depression. One of the most trying things in the Icelandic economic world just now is that they cannot get their dried fish sold in Spain. The herring trade is also in rather a difficult position. But when we talked of poverty and trade depression someone told me that there was never in Iceland such a depth of degradation as one can find in an English slum. There is so much land to spare in Iceland that anyone can scratch a living from it. Moreover, there is always the sea with its plentiful supply of fish. So, though the conditions of

life may be hard, for no-one in Iceland is there danger
of absolute starvation.

So we chatted until we saw steam rising in the distance,
and there, in a perfectly bleak landscape, lying in the
hollow of the bleak hills, was a little group of glass houses
wreathed in steam. We walked through groves of
tomatoes, plantations of cucumbers, houses of rather
frail roses, and beds of melons. The warmth of the
natural spring was very grateful after the dank cold of the
atmosphere outside. Then we went up to see the parents
of the proprietor.[7] They were a charming old couple —
the father in working clothes and rope shoes, the old lady
almost blind but holding herself erect, her bust firmly
laced into the corset of the national dress. The little
beret, with its long tassel, was perched coquettishly on
her head, and she had beautiful ornaments of filigree on
her bodice. We drank coffee, and they discussed politics
with vigour but with perfect courtesy.

Then we went on to an open-air swimming-bath,
supplied by one of the hot springs. The water was
pleasantly tepid, though the effort of undressing and
getting in under the rainy sky was considerable. We
had more coffee, this time with the proprietor of the
woollen factory which stands quite near.[8] The factory is
run from the hot springs. Further the houses in the
district use the spring water for central heating and for
all ordinary purposes. It is so hot that tea can be made
from it directly with no further boiling.

I spent a nice evening with some Icelandic friends.
We discussed the national character. I said it was a
peculiar experience to come to this country knowing
nothing of the people but what I had learnt from the
sagas. I had expected to find Iceland populated by

---

[7] Probably Ásgeir Bjarnason and Ragnheiður Helgadóttir, the parents of Bjarni Ásgeirsson, the co-owner of the greenhouses at Reykir in Mosfellssveit.

[8] Sigurjón Pétursson (1885–1955), another *glíma* champion who ran the Álafoss cloth factory.

those portentous figures, Gudrun of the Laxdale Saga, Egill Skallagrimsson, Viga-Glum. I had expected the most striking characteristics to be a sort of stiffness of character and a high degree of offendability. Instead of that I find the most civilized people in Europe, whose manners combine absolute courtesy to a stranger without any of the tiresome fussing or curiosity that often accompanies hospitality. I had noticed, however, that the people in the shops were a little unencouraging at first and seemed almost to resent your wanting to buy anything. But when I persisted they thawed and became eager to get me what I wanted. One of the party thought that the attitude of the shop people was due to pride and that pride is a very important quality in the Icelander. It is that which makes them dislike cadging for money, so the Icelander is always unwilling to over-charge. I was able to observe this phenomenon later, when I was riding in the country. When I asked one of the farmers how much I owed him for hire of horses and hospitality, he sat fingering his chin and, after some consideration, said "Twenty-five *krónur*". I thanked him and handed him the money, which represented a very reasonable charge. He took it and sat a few moments with it in his hand. Then he took a five-*krónur* note and gave it to me, saying, "No, I think I've charged you too much. Twenty *krónur* is enough." And this in a country where money is not too easily come by. The Icelander's pride is also the basis for his courage and power of suffering discomforts without complaints. I was told that at the celebrations of the millenary of the Althing the beds in the tents allotted to students had got damp. That, I thought, was in itself characteristic. I didn't find the Icelander a very practical person. The Norwegian and the Swedish students panicked on the grounds that they would catch cold. The Icelandic students slept in the damp beds and caught cold uncomplainingly.

Another of the party suggested that the kindness and

at the same time the lack of fussing had been developed by the farm life, i.e., that through the centuries the Icelanders had had to do with animals. It is an interesting theory that the Icelandic pony has tamed his fierce and uncompromising master. But the ponies themselves are tamed. I heard a funny story of the horse-fight that was to be shown at the millenary celebrations. There were many protests against the revival of this barbarous form of sport. But because it was traditional and of the Saga Age, the fight was held. But when the ponies were put to it, instead of biting with concentrated hatred, they rolled and played like a couple of puppies. The promoters of the fight had unfortunately picked on two firm friends, who enjoyed a good romp together.

Next morning I went out to Thingvellir, the plain where the first national parliament was held a thousand years ago. The car passed through desolate hills of monotonous and craggy outline until I wondered when we should arrive at the rocky ridge of the Almannagjá. Then we saw a lake to the right, Thingvallavatn, and skirting the edge we arrived at the craggy ridge down which the road runs between high cliffs.[9] We descended to the plain and made a large circuit to cross the river and arrive at the hotel.

Thingvellir is very beautiful and the formation of the rocks extraordinary. Sometimes they split, forming deep clefts filled with blue-green water. This is so clear that the floating weeds look like jewels. Above the lava plain is the ridge where the meetings were held. I scrambled about looking for the *lögberg* and the famous booths. There is no difficulty finding these as they are conveniently marked by tablets. The view from the ridge is exquisite, the river Oxará in the foreground with

---

[9] The classic description of the approach to the parliament ground at Þingvellir is to be found in Lord Dufferin, *Letters from High Latitudes* (1856), ch. VII.

the "holm" or island on which the famous duel between Gunnlaug Ormstunga and Hrafn was fought "for the love of a lady", then, across that, the church and the vicarage, a grey house with a bright green roof, which proved on closer examination to be of growing turf. Beyond stretches the lava plain, humping itself uneasily into little wrinkles, but covered between the rocks with grass, scrub and little birch trees. In the far distance the mountains stand blue in the morning sunshine, still wearing their winter caps of snow. It was from the shield-shaped Skjaldbreið that the red hot lava poured in distant ages, which was to cool, and harden, and form a stage for some of the most remarkable events in Icelandic history.[10]

I walked past the waterfalls along to the edge of the ridge, through the sweet-scented scrub birch. Snow was still lying in the shaded crannies of the ravine. Then I struck across the heath. It was very desolate and very lovely, with no life but the plovers, which whined round me with a persistence that soon became irritating. Then it began to rain, so I turned back and examined the little church and graveyard across Oxará. It was settling down to rain with more conviction now, so I went back to the hotel and drank coffee. I was smoking a cigarette and gazing out rather drearily into the grey and desolate monotony of the plain, when a car drove up to the hotel, and another, and another, till the plain was desolate no longer and the solitudes were filled with young students. The girls were trying to be reckless, and the boys were most of them tipsy, carrying bottles, shouting, kissing, singing, dancing and, it seemed to me, ignoring the young women. One young man practised his English on me and told me that they had passed their

[10] Skjaldbreið: this mountain is well known on the skyline from Þingvellir. During the whole of the last century it was generally assumed to be the source of the lava which forms the floor of Þingvellir. Regretfully we must now accept the more modern theory that most of the lava came from fissures to the east of Skjaldbreið. See B. Thorsteinsson and Th. Josepsson, *Thingvellir* (1961), 8.

matriculation into the university and were celebrating their entrance into student life. He told me (I suspect untruthfully) that he was going to be a clergyman and that he would have few opportunities in the future of enjoying himself in this particular way. He introduced a great many of his friends, who were all very distinguished. One was the best orator of the year, another the best mathematician, and so on. I thought the boys and girls were trying very hard to enjoy themselves, but even whilst I was there I noticed that their spirits flagged. They were to spend the night out there at the hotel, and I wondered if it would be long before they could return to Reykjavik and sleep off their aching heads. The weather was, of course, depressing. I suppose things would go with more snap in the sunshine.

I went home in a car with an earnest young German from Kiel, who wanted to improve his English. I wanted to improve my German, but he won.

The next day I spent at the Library and Museum. In the Museum I saw clothes, woven fabrics and above all carved wooden objects. There were carved wood cupboards, food-bowls, spoon-boxes, cake moulds, and even wringer handles. I suppose the long winter evenings are so boring that the men in the country decorate every available wooden surface with carving. I pictured Mother restraining them from carving the rollers of the wringer.

I had tea with an unsuccessful Labour candidate at the last election.[11] She is a large woman, intensely idealistic, and belonging to all sorts of International Leagues of Women, except the National Council. She sat there with her hat askew and her stockings wrinkling to the ankle.

In the evening I was to meet the same lady with a group of others for dinner. I saw a tall, fair, stately

---

[11] Laufey Valdimarsdóttir (1890–1945) was the daughter of Briet Bjarnhéðinsdóttir, the most famous of Iceland's suffragettes.

woman coming forward with dignity to meet me in the hotel. It was the same lady in national costume. Often during my stay in Iceland I was to see this extraordinary metamorphosis. Some school-girl slut in a bedraggled cotton frock would appear as a woman with poise and experience, only because she had changed into her national dress. The tightly laced corset forces the wearer to stand or sit erect and the long skirt gives dignity, while the little beret and the plaited hair are worn with an attractive air of coquetry. It was a little group of university women who composed our dinner party. It was a gay dinner, pretty dresses, a bottle of Sauterne, and a great deal of chattering and laughter. But they grow very serious when they talk of their country. They said that the Althing millenary was the greatest experience of their lives, and that the Icelanders who were present felt that not only a great past was behind them but that a great future lay ahead. That was their moment, when they had faith in Iceland's future. They said they had forgotten that faith later, especially with the fury of the election, but they had their moment and it was worth while.

What else did we talk about? Trifles mostly. The lady who felt that she had once been a lamb in Svarfadardale.[12] The ponies (at the millenary celebrations) that refused to fight. I asked if the University Women in Reykjavik gossiped and said unpleasant things about each other. They thought not, partly because there were so few of them, partly because they were united by their sense of pioneerdom. They had all been first in some field — one the first girl to enter the High School, one the first woman teacher in the school. One was the first government clerk, one the first to own a chemist's shop, and so on.[13]

[12] Aðalbjörg Sigurðardóttir (b. 1887), a well-known suffragette and theosophist.
[13] The first Icelandic woman to graduate from Reykjavík High School was Laufey Valdimarsdóttir, see note 11; the first woman government clerk was Ásta Magnúsdóttir who entered government service in 1910; Jóhanna Magnúsdóttir was the first to own a chemist's shop, which she started in 1928.

My boat was to leave that night for the north, so the gay little group saw me off in the now persistent rain.

The next day wore away. The unfriendly mountains were hidden in the mist and the unfriendly sea bickered round our little boat. The boat was crowded. Many of the passengers were being rather vocally sea-sick in their berths. A few of us huddled in the smokeroom. Someone was playing a gramophone, and we tried to make a tight little defence of human civilization against the void that lay outside.

Snow was falling on the mountains, but it turned to rain as it reached the fjord. The sea was rough, and I slept. When I woke it was calmer and we were creeping into Isafjord. It looked a grim place, packed onto a spit of land lying across the fjord. The mountains rise almost sheer from the water, and in the winter for nearly two months the little town is cut off from the sunlight. Then, in January when the first rays of the sun strike the town, the people drink coffee and eat cakes to celebrate.

We had a few hours to wait. I picked my way through the puddles of the street to pay a call. The place should have been romantic with the quays lined with brown-sailed boats full of sea-birds' eggs; but the rain and mud were as unromantic as they are in England. I went along a little gully to the mainland, where a road leads along the fjord. In a nice white house at the foot of the mountains lives the clergyman.[14] He is charming, intellectual, and was unflurried by the arrival of a visitor who dislocated the family dinner and drank coffee at an inconvenient hour. He talked Icelandic to me with the utmost patience, articulating every syllable, as did his son, Siggi litli. His two small, square, red girls were too shy to talk to the English lady. He had a lot of books, the Icelandic sagas, and a collection of English books on

---

[14] Sigurgeir Sigurðsson (1890–1953) became Bishop of Iceland on 1 January 1939. His two daughters were called Svanhildur and Guðlaug.

Spiritualism, mainly by the Rev. Vale Owen.[15] Then I called on the doctor whose little girls entertained me with courtesy and self-possession.[16]

That evening we were in the Arctic circle and should have seen the Midnight Sun, but it rained, so I had a bath and went to bed. Next day the weather showed faint signs of improvement. By the time we had passed Skagafjord and Drangey, where the outlaw Grettir found peace, the sun was out, and we arrived at Siglufjord on a glorious summer day.

I had heard a great deal about Siglufjord, a place of bad aroma both literally and metaphorically. I had been told that it was the only place in Iceland where a solitary woman is not perfectly safe. It is the centre of the herring industry and hence famous at certain times of the year for its bad smell. Fortunately the herring season had not yet begun.

The place certainly looked nasty. There were squashed fish and squashed birds on the quay, a great many sinister-looking men in the streets, and a not too obtrusive smell of fish-oil. The country round is lovely. I climbed up a bit of one of the mountains and had a magnificent view of the fjord and the town, which is not unpicturesque when seen from a height. Then the steamer's whistle blew, and we were soon rounding Siglunes and passing into Eyjafjord. The sun shone, the sea was blue and the mountain tops were white with snow.

---

[15] George Vale Owen (1869–1931) published several books on the after-life in the 1920s.
[16] Vilmundur Jónsson (1889–1972) became Iceland's Chief Medical Officer of Health in October 1931. His daughters were Guðrún and Ólöf.

Chapter Two

AKUREYRI AND EYJAFJORD

EYJAFJORD is one of the loveliest fjords in Iceland. The chief place is Akureyri, the largest town in Iceland after Reykjavik. It lies almost at the top of the fjord. To the left, just before it is reached, there is a range of mountains of the characteristic pyramid shape, which always reminded me of a row of ice-puddings with the top sliced off. It is an agreeable little town, with several comfortable hotels, two picture theatres and a very fine modern store belonging to the Co-operative Association. This large new building is the first thing that the visitor sees when he walks up from the quay. Behind the town the ground rises, and after a twenty minutes' walk you reach the foot of Sulur, the mountain that stands at the back of the town. Out into the fjord there is a spit of land where the small boats come in. Along the fjord the land is flat, and here is the fish-drying ground. Then there is a large factory before you come to Glerá, a river which supplies the town with electricity. Beyond that there is a working-class area of houses and a sort of suburb. Up the fjord on the hill behind the town the houses are more imposing. They are for the most part nice new villas and often have gardens with flowers growing in them. The other houses have all their patch of grass railed off from the road by wire fencing, but the owners cultivate the grass for hay and do not attempt any horticulture. Up the hill there is even a public garden, which stands next to the school. It is gay with columbines and valerian. Here also are trees, little birch bushes, none of them growing more than five or six feet high; but the people of Akureyri are very proud of their wooded park. On the lower road along the fjord there is a quay with stacks of wood and barrels; these are followed by a district of smaller houses and a fish-drying ground. Here the men put out their nets and I found it fascinating to watch them dragging in the nets and flinging out the poor protesting fish with which they seemed always to be full. Another interest of this road that flanked the fjord was the families of eider-duck which swam near the edge. The fathers, I was told, took no further interest in their children after the hatching was over, but escaped to the sea where they enjoyed their bachelorhood together, leaving the mothers to their parental responsibilities. The down with which the nests are lined used to be a very valuable commodity in Iceland, and a farmer who owned a nesting-ground on the flats near the fjord was a fortunate person. But now the trade has dwindled because of the cost of collecting and cleaning the down.

Akureyri has an open-air swimming bath. It forms a very nice social centre, and though it is only the children and the more intrepid males who venture into its icy water, a great many people of both sexes sit about on the grass banks and watch the bathers. I was amused to read the first time I went that the bath was reserved for women at that particular time and to observe that the only people in it were men and boys. After that I stopped taking much notice of the printed word. Another thing that contributes to the gaiety of Akureyri is the Herdubreid Café. This was just opposite the window of my bedroom, and as there was a dance almost every night that I was there, I could watch the dancers arriving and leaving, and listen from my bed to the music of the jazz band. The place was often very gay as many boats called at Akureyri, and their sailors patronised the Herdubreid.

The arrival of the boats is the most exciting thing in Akureyri, for all letters and parcels come by boat and not by road. The day that the boat is due the excitement begins to simmer. You ask each other when "Dettifoss" or "Godafoss" is due. Then you begin to argue about it, and someone tells you that they heard from the postmaster that she left Isafjord that morning. Then, perhaps, you hear the steamer's whistle as she comes up the fjord. You hurry out to see her come in, to meet your friends, to "goup" if you are to be merely an onlooker. She draws nearer and gradually, with a good deal of shouting and blowing of whistles, she creeps alongside the quay. You wave at your friends or scan the faces of the visitors. The gangway is put down and you hurry on board, come off laughing and chattering with your friends, carrying luggage and paper-bags or flowers from Reykjavik. The next excitement is the post. You have a key with which you can obtain your letters even though the post office is shut. So the street echoes to the hurrying steps, and round the post office there is a little crowd. Next morning the parcels have been unshipped, and the pavements in front of the shops are cluttered with wooden packing-cases. Then the windows are gay with the latest models from Copenhagen, and the tobacconist has a new supply of oranges. After the boat leaves the town sinks into torpor, until the next boat is due.

The hotel I stayed in was kept by an ex-housekeeper from the hospital.[17] She is the Mrs Beaton of Iceland and has written a cookery book which I was told was on the way to becoming a classic. Certainly she was an excellent cook; the food was delicious and a good advertisement for her book. For lunch, I remember, on the first day we had a soufflé served in coquilles, trout with fried onions, and an exquisite cream made with tinned fruit. The chief draw-back for those not used to pension life in the Scandinavian countries is the ordeal of coming into the dining room and finding one's place at the long table, lined on either side with strangers. It is the most harrowing experience imaginable, especially when one is

---

[17] Jóninna Sigurðardóttir (b. 1879). Her cookery book, first published in 1915, has gone through several editions.

aware that some sort of conventional greeting is expected from a newcomer, and one is not sure what the exact form is. It was some time before I acquired the right formula, *verði yður að góðu* ("may it do you good"). I used to murmur "God bless you" and trust that it would pass. Further problems arise when you are not sure of the exact sequence of the meal. The supper consisted of a hot course followed by a variety of cold objects of the nature of hors d'œuvres. But many of the inmates used to take a preliminary snack from these for they were all ready on the table. If one began like this one was immediately embarrassed by the arrival of the maid, who pressed hot meat and potatoes on you. Then, of course, all the most agreeable of the cold objects were out of range, and one did not know their names even in English, still less in Icelandic, and one was too shy, and too well brought up, to stretch or point.

This hotel was admirable in other matters. The rooms were plainly furnished and the walls painted with light grey washable paint. There was running water (but, alas, only cold) in all the rooms. There was a bathroom and central heating. The proprietress was kindly and the maid charming. She was rather sorry for me and suspected I was lonely. She used to come to my room in the evenings, when I was reading or writing, and talk to me patiently in Icelandic or, sometimes when I couldn't understand, in Danish. I remember one evening when an Englishman, who had been on the boat with me, got drunk and made a speech from the steps of the Herdubreid, that she came running up to my room to tell me and we peered together through the curtains and made the sort of shocked noises with our tongues that are common to all languages.

One evening I went to a play in Akureyri and there found the proprietress and the maid. They insisted I should sit by them and further, in the interval, asked me to take coffee with them and pressed cakes on me, for which they paid. I had a picture in my mind of the conventional boarding-house keeper in England.

On my first visit I stayed only one night in Akureyri as I was being accompanied to Svarfadardale next day. The first evening in Akureyri was notable for me, in that I didn't quite see the Midnight Sun. We were told that we should see it from Sulur, but I didn't climb high enough and at 11.50 it disappeared behind a mountain. It certainly was a remarkably beautiful sunset, and it was a curious experience to creep home in the pink glow to find the town sleeping, the hotel locked up, and to wonder whether I was returning too late at night or too early in the morning.

The next day I left for Svarfadardale by motor-boat in company with the clergyman and his family.[18] We were to leave early in the morning, then it was to be at one, but the afternoon wore slowly away and it was six o'clock before the overloaded little boat got under way. The journey was not very comfortable as the small boat held Séra Stefán and his family, the crew and the owner and his friends, our luggage, a wooden door, hay rakes, sacks of rye, barrels and three rolls of barbed wire. The elder ladies wrapped shawls round their heads and disappeared into the tiny cabin. The rest of us perched on sacks and barrels and ate buns out of paper bags. Séra Stefán and his daughter removed the more external of their town clothes and struggled into oil skins and rubber boots. It was bitterly cold and spiteful little waves splashed over the side. After about four hours we arrived at Dalvik, the little fishing port of Svarfadardale. There is nothing but a cluster of houses, mostly new. The quay or quays, for there are two of them, fragile wooden structures, stretch out into the fjord and have a rusty truck-line down the middle. They are lined

---

[18] Séra Stefán Kristinsson was priest at Vellir from 1901 to 1941. His wife was Solveig Pétursdóttir Eggerz and his two daughters were named Ingibjörg and Sigríður.

with a grim array of fishes' heads, drying to be ground
down into fishmeal. It is rather like the religious house
in a Melanesian village — set on piles with ranks of
grinning skulls.

We shivered on the quay whilst the boat was unloaded.
There were a great many more things than I had been
aware of — boxes, trunks and paper bags, Ingibjorg's
clothes hanging rather insecurely on coat-hangers, a
cistern, a lavatory basin, some drain pipes, a large iron
object — probably a boiler, and a jam jar with a rose
cutting in it. While these were being unpacked
Ingibjorg's friends, two pretty girls in berets, were
dancing around and giggling, delighted at the re-union,
for she had been away for a year teaching gymnastics
in Reykjavik.

I was led up the quay and along the village street. A
wide valley opened up to the south with snow-tipped
mountains on each side with a range shutting in the top
of the dale. A wide and rather swift-flowing river wound
through the flat green bottom. The mountain peaks
were flushed with pink from a sun low over the fjords,
and up the gently sloping sides of the valley, below the
precipitous mountains, was a scattering of little white
farms.

We were taken to the beret-girls' home and beside the
grateful warmth of an electric radiator were given cold
milk and cake. Nature's needs were satisfied in a bedroom
with the help of a chamber perched rather insecurely
on a feather bed.

Then a motor lorry came along. The goods from the
quay had been collected and increased by the addition
of a huge bunch of fish — trout and some big flat ones
which were still jumping convulsively as a protest against
their translation into another element. Mrs Stefán
climbed in the front. Sera Stefán, Ingibjorg and I sat
rather insecurely on the boxes behind, the driver got
in, and a supernumerary clung to the mudguard. Then

we jolted off, swinging along what was a comparatively
good road. After a mile or so we turned over the
narrowest possible bridge and followed a cart track over
the river flats, then another bridge, followed by more
cart track. The river here is in four or five branches
and at the last we had to transfer into a boat. Across
the river there was a black fluffy dog called Snati, which
was barking a hysterical welcome to the family. A boy
was waiting with a long two-wheeled cart and a pony.
We climbed up the side of the valley for half a mile or so
and reached Vellir.

It is a white house of corrugated iron, lined with wood;
rather like a double-fronted villa, with a flight of steps
to the front door. It is the parsonage and close by there
is a tiny white, green-roofed church. Round this there
is an old graveyard, raised from the ground by a slight
mound; but busy feet do not respect its sanctity for it
makes a short cut from the house to the river. There
is also a new graveyard, which is fenced in and has a
row of mountain ashes and one of these brave
attempts at a garden — a row of lupins and poppies, all
rather bleached by the cruel wind.

I haven't yet described the clergyman and his wife.
He is bearded like an apostle and has a brown, weather-
beaten face with surprising light grey eyes. He was a
fisherman in his youth and has the slightly slouching
shoulders that are often a sign of great strength. He
spits a great deal. He is evidently a wag, though I
couldn't understand his jokes. On the boat he had
struggled into a pair of light blue dungarees, put on some
leather leggings and a yellow oilskin coat, and when he
had finished he seemed a much more convincing country
prestur than the respectable, brown-suited gentleman
that I had met on the "Godafoss". Clergymen in
Iceland wear no uniform in ordinary life. When they
conduct the services they wear black cassocks and the
sweetest frills or ruffs round their necks. Mrs Stefán

is fat and has a nice homely face. In Akureyri she was
wearing the national dress, black and close-fitting, with
a coloured silk apron and a huge white satin bow on her
bosom. Her hair was plaited in several plaits and looped
up under the little beret with its dangling tassel. Over
this costume she wore an ordinary raincoat. In the house
she wears a cotton frock that has no distinctive national
qualities, and she wears her grey plaits down her back.
The daughter, Ingibjorg, is a modern — a little athletic
thing who whistles, strides like a boy, and despises the
national costume.

When we reached the door of the house my hostess
turned to me with a kindly "Welcome to Vellir". We
went into the front room, where the table was laid for a
meal — horn-handled knives, black and white bread, a
large block of butter, and a large jug of milk. I enjoyed
the meal, for it was now one in the morning and, except for
a bun or two on the boat and the milk at Dalvik, I had
had nothing since lunch. We had veal stew with potatoes
and boiled eggs and then porridge and milk. After supper
I waited out in the sunset-dawn till my bag was brought
up from the river. There was a smell of dew, and a smell
of peat smoke. It was cold and peaceful except for a
curlew which was whining with its mate down in the
grass near the river.

The parlour upstairs had been turned into my bedroom
with pillows, sheets and duvet on the couch. There was
a bowl of cold water and a piece of soap on the polished
table for my toilet.

About ten the next morning there was a knock at the
door, and the younger daughter, a pretty dark girl with
two long plaits of hair, came in carrying a large copper
kettle of coffee, a jug of cream, and a trayful of cakes.
This was my first experience of the little breakfast that
was always brought to me in bed in Iceland. At first it
is a shade disconcerting to meet the fancy biscuits and
cakes with layers of jam at such an early meal.

Sometimes the fragile and delicious pancakes that are such a feature of coffee parties were brought. But I came to enjoy my morning snack, and the coffee was always strong, hot and freshly made, and the cream delicious. I was often so ashamed at the gaps that I had made in the inevitable tray of cakes that I used to re-arrange them on the tray and trust that my hostess did not check the numbers.

Too soon for one to be really hungry again, we sat down to lunch — yesterday's stew and some of the fish that had ridden with us in the lorry the night before. My hostess told me about their life. The salary of a clergyman is negligible, so they live by farming. At Vellir they have nine cows and three calves, hence the delicious milk, cream, butter, cheese and *skyr*. This is the national dish, sour milk, which has been strained and beaten till it is like whipped cream. It is eaten with sugar and cream. It is supposed to be essential to health and to supply the deficiencies that would otherwise show in the Icelandic diet because of the lack of fresh fruit and vegetables.

The housewife at Vellir is out at seven every morning to see to the dairy work. Then there are the sheep — not very many because the grazing is not good and the *tún* small. They have some meadows down near the river for the hay. But they spin the wool from the sheep and make it into stockings for the children, and they wear home-spun and knitted things in the winter. In summer they have shop-made clothes.

Meals at Vellir are continuous. When I was there, there were twenty mouths to feed, including the ten men and women who work on the estate and an additional group of workmen who were building a house for the eldest son. The bread is home-made, the meat is home-grown and home-killed, and the smoked fish and meat are home-cured. Except for the coffee, sugar, flour and condiments, everything can be produced on the estate.

During the week I was at Vellir I walked and rode up and down Svarfadardale, which is about twenty miles long, and Skidadale, which is a tributary dale about the same length. I wanted to see the places mentioned in the saga of the men of Svarfadardale.

It is better to ride in the dale than to walk. The streams are sometimes too deep and too swift to cross safely on foot, even when you are wearing rubber boots. But the ponies pick their way through the torrent with careful security, turning the heads upstream so that they will not be carried out of their course by the current. My first experience of riding was unalarming. The younger daughter from Vellir was my guide, a lovely girl, grave, reserved and kindly. She led the way at a gentle walk, increased later to a trot and finally a mild canter. The ponies are surer-footed on the steep slopes of the river bank than I should have been myself. In an emergency I clung to the mane. Once I found myself clinging round the neck, but that was before I had mastered the elementary rule of safety that going uphill the rider should lean forward, and going downhill the weight should be put back. After this fact was learned I was never even near to falling off.

During my week in Svarfadardale the weather grew steadily worse. At first it was bright but cold. Then it grew cloudy, and then the rain began. After that it grew still colder, the rain turned to snow and sleet, and the bitterest wind blew unceasingly. My first impression of the Icelandic countryside was one of complete gloom. The north wind whistled round the house. The grass was green, but in rather a subdued way. In the little churchyard at Vellir there were a few Iceland poppies, and I used to go out and warm my eyes with the red and yellow flowers. Everything else seemed bleak and cold. The river was a cold blue, the mountains colourless, except their tips, which were outlined in hard snow. The mountain sides take their colour from the sky; in dull weather they are a neutral shade, greenish with huge stretches of yellowish sand, greyish rock and scree. It is only in the sunlight they become lovely, an indescribable blue, and the shadows from the little clouds chase across their slopes.

As I walked alone in the dale I used to contemplate Nature with a certain fear. Iceland seemed to me like a great animal, brooding and but half tamed. She is always hitching herself uneasily into wrinkles, and unless these are regularly smoothed by the hard-working farmer the surface of the fields became covered with little grassy humps. Sometimes there are bigger disturbances — volcanic eruptions or avalanches — so that in a few hours the whole face of the countryside is changed.

I think that my fear of the country was due to the fact that a vulgarian like myself should have been introduced to this undiluted Nature rather more gradually. Never before have I been brought into such close contact with such extensive stretches of Nature. In most of the countries I had travelled in I had seen the wilds in company or from the security of a steamer, a railway train or a motor car. Again, I was always hungry, and I was too shy to go to the farms and ask for coffee. I thought with longing of a walking tour in the Tyrol where one was as likely as not to find a nice little café round the next corner with check table-cloths and cream cakes. And I knew that round the next corner in these dales I should see only the grass slopes and the uncomprehending mountain sides. Even the animals seemed unfriendly, and no wonder in this land fretted by a bitter wind, with the June snow lying unmelted in the hollows. I was knocked down by a bull calf, snapped at by farm dogs, menaced by the sea swallows when I went too near their breeding grounds. Even the sheep were hostile and shook their horns at me until I was driven to creep round the other way.

I remember that on the Friday I was there I walked out

along the dale to the fjord; quite suddenly I came on a new road on which about a dozen men and boys were working. I felt cheered by the proximity of so much humanity and lingered there as long as I could. The road was rather casually constructed with a bed of turfs and a top surface of stones and boulders. Already the waters of the fjord were beating against its side, and I wondered how long it would be before the greedy waves had licked away this new link with civilization.

On my way home that evening I walked with a man in blue dungarees, and we chatted with some difficulty. When we drew near the farm where he lived, he led me out of the way to a sheltered hollow and showed me a little village of toy houses made by children from the farm. The tiny mud houses were roofed with turf and fenced with sheep's horns. There were flowers, daisies and little pink arenaria planted in the gardens, and there was even a cemetery with crosses made from match sticks. I felt unaccountably cheered.

That night the wind howled round the house and the sleet beat on the tiny windows of my bedroom. I had been given a little bedroom to myself, at the expense of poor Ingibjorg, who would normally have slept there. The mystery of how the family, servants and guests were housed in a house no larger than a villa was only incompletely solved for me during the whole of my stay in Iceland. The *baðstofa* houses most of the servants; but where the family pack themselves away was a thing I never understood. My bedroom conformed to what was a common type. It was a little, wood-lined room and its ceiling sloped down almost to the floor so that in my bed under the eaves I was in danger of hitting my head on the roof. The walls and floor were painted, the bedstead was a white wooden one with boards underneath, a straw underlay, a feather mattress and on top a feather duvet which was always slipping off. I slept in two jerseys. There was a tiny washstand, a chair, a quantity of photographs, Christmas cards, picture post-cards, and some small china objects.

Icelandic interiors are seldom distinguished. The furniture is uninteresting, and there is nothing characteristic except a litter of photographs, the Nottingham lace curtains and a row of plants on the window-sill. But the kitchens of the smaller old turf and timber houses often have beautiful wooden furniture — chests and boxes in white wood or gaily painted. The lack of distinction in the newer furnishing dates from the time when the farmers built their new houses but had not yet emerged far in taste beyond the kitchen or *baðstofa*. So when they had new rooms, parlours and bedrooms to furnish, they bought the first furniture they saw in the town store. Further they were, and still are, circumscribed in their choice and have to depend on the shopkeepers, who have neither the taste nor the capital to stock a large variety of furniture.

It rained or sleeted all that day. I spent it in the pleasant warmth of the best room, where the stove had been lighted. It was *laugardagur* — Saturday which means washing-day — when everything is being cleaned in readiness for Sunday. Floors were being washed, clean curtains put up and the family washing and ironing was being done. As it was so wet the women were in from the fields and all busy about the house. We sat in the dining-room and drank coffee. The *húsfreyja* comes in with a fresh pot of coffee, we fill our cups and the conversation grows animated. They are talking of life after death, and in the warm little room, with the wind howling and the snow falling on the misty mountains, they discuss whether they would be afraid to see their dead friends. The *húsfreyja*, her broad face flushed from the kitchen, sips her coffee and thinks that there is nothing to be frightened of. Ingibjorg, modern and disrespectful, says something in her incisive way, and they all laugh. The Pastor, his spectacles pushed up on his forehead, is ranging up and down the room as if he was on the deck of a boat, and now and then he pauses to tap the barometer or to peer through the steamy window panes. The workwomen, glad enough to sit passive, stir the dregs in their cups. A boy comes in with a message, his face glowing from the cold and an airman's helmet pulled down over his flaxen hair.

The *húsfreyja* shows me the house. We pass through the kitchen or *eldhús*, where a woman is frying some sort of crumpet or fritter over the peat stove. Then we pass along a turf passage, roofed with wood, into the *baðstofa*. This is new, but has been built on the site of the old one and on the old model. It is a three-roomed compartment. In the left-hand room sit the girls and in the right-hand one the men. In the middle room live an old couple, pensioners, who chaperon and keep the young people in order. The beds are old wooden ones, smoothed and polished with generations of handling. On the beds are brown blankets spun and woven from the wool of the Vellir sheep. When they are not more actively employed the girls sit on their beds and spin and weave, though now the price of labour is so high that it is cheaper to buy materials and clothes ready-made from Scotland and Sweden. I saw the spinning wheels and wool winders. The old couple, almost blind with age, were sitting on their beds in the middle room. The old lady was plaiting wool and crooning to herself. The old man had a white beard and was wearing a blue jersey.

Then I was taken to the *fjós* to see where the cows and horses lived. The *fjós* is made of turfs and has double doors; it seems warm and comfortable with the sweet smell of the cows. Each of the cows has a name — Brynja, Flora, and so on.

That wet day I had no cause to complain of hunger. I had coffee in bed, lunch at ten-thirty, and coffee and cakes at one. Then in the afternoon about five an unexpected and supererogatory meal appeared, excused,

I suppose, because of the cold weather. It was chocolate and *lummur*, the little thick pancakes that I'd seen being fried in the kitchen. I had three distinct varieties of pancakes or doughnuts in Iceland: (a) *pönnukökur*, little thin pancakes which are rolled and eaten with sugar, jam and sometimes whipped cream, (b) *kleinur*, little twisted pieces of dough fried in deep fat and dusted with sugar, and (c) *lummur*, or thick fritters. It was these we ate that afternoon. They had been made as a treat for the men who were working at the building in the rain, but we insiders also benefited. At seven I had little appetite for the dinner of fish and *hangikjöt*, or smoked mutton, which is not very nice, because the rank taste of the decaying meat is distinguishable through the flavour of smoke. There was also *harðfiskur*, the dried cod which is considered a dainty. You smear it with butter and poke a shred in your mouth, then chew, and chew, and chew. After some hard work there is a quite perceptible flavour on your palate, but the experience did not seem to me altogether to justify the labour involved. It is used a lot as a snack, on picnics or on riding tours, and also serves as hors d'oeuvres or a titbit to amuse yourself with while waiting for the next course.

After dinner I helped to take things down from the parlour to the kitchen. In the downstairs dining-room there was an animated scene. The work people were at dinner. Séra Stefán was sitting at the head of the table, his face curiously refined in contrast with the wind-flushed faces of the workers, who were sitting three on either side. They were all in dungarees and coarse home-spun shirts. Elbows on the table, they were intent on shovelling porridge into their mouths. The table was littered with large bones, which were picked so clean that I suspect that it was not only knives and forks that had been used. At the foot of the table was a small boy, an adopted son of the house. Round the room were one or two other men, puffing at their pipes so that the air was blue with smoke. The old man and woman from the *baðstofa* were there, she with her wrinkled face, glazed blind eyes and two plaits of ungreyed hair. The gramophone was being worked by a tousle-headed young man and was grinding out alternately comic songs and religious music. Then the flaxen-haired boy came in carrying a plate, knife and fork, and a dish of meat and potatoes. He started in solidly, shovelling the butter onto his plate from the common dish. Another boy came in and elbowed his way to a place at the table.

After dinner an entertainment was promised us. The table was pushed back and a space cleared in the middle of the room. Round the walls sat or leant the red-faced men in blue, their hair ruffled and their pipes bubbling. The women from the kitchen, their hair in plaits and red handkerchiefs over their heads, crowded in the doorway. The *húsfreyja* sat proud and placid, and the little children played under the table. Then Ingibjorg came in wearing a blue bathing dress and gave a gymnastic display, contorting her lithe body as a spectacle for twenty pairs of eyes. In such a way would such an audience have watched the saga heroes at their wrestling, and all the time the gramophone played "Nearer my God to Thee".

Then we had another coffee party to celebrate the wet Saturday and the general feeling of festivity. We all sat round the table, Séra Stefán, his wife, the girls, the working-men, the women from the kitchen, and the old couple from the *baðstofa*. The coffee was served from an elegant brass pot, which was too small and dripped on to the table cloth. These Icelanders have a sweet tooth. After the cakes and biscuits they fancy a lump of sugar dipped in coffee, and that evening I saw many surreptitious and rather dirty hands stretch out towards the sugar bowl.

Chapter Three

AKUREYRI AGAIN AND A JOURNEY TO THE EAST

THE next morning I left Svarfadardale, paying an absurdly small amount for the hospitality. I had a long and rather tiring walk to Fagriskógur where I was to be picked up by a car and taken to Akureyri. It rained a great deal, and I had two heavy rucksacks to carry. I had a rest from my burdens when a boy on a horse stopped and offered to carry them as far as he was going. He made conversation so nicely to me. After Stærriárskógur the track grew wilder and less clearly defined, and wandered among bleak hills, whose sides were covered with scree. The mists came lower so that the tips of even the lowest hills were shrouded. Horned sheep threatened me from across bogs and I thought that I was on the wrong road. There was no one to ask. I wished for Sigurd's gift of tongues so that I could ask the way of a curlew. Then the old track vanished altogether, and I was in despair. But it was not for long, for I soon saw in the distance a row of stakes that indicated a new road. After that it was more cheerful. I balanced precariously on a plank over a ravine and soon arrived at a fine new house where I was to meet the car. It was the home of one of Iceland's famous poets,[19] but I did not meet any of the family as they were all out on some Sunday jaunt. A maid received me kindly, helped me off with my muddy boots, and I was grateful to sit in a little room, sipping coffee and to hear the wind blowing outside and to see the new fallen snow on the top of the mountain just

---

[19] Davíð Stefánsson frá Fagraskógi (1895–1964), poet, playwright and novelist.

outside the window. I smoked my last cigarette and felt at peace.

All the clocks in Iceland are wrong. The maid told me that the car would arrive at ten, by their clock, which was two and a half hours fast. I learnt later that there were two times — "telephone time" which is the right one, and "country time" which is settled by the individual farmer. It's a sort of daylight saving and often a device of the farmers to get more work out of his people. I heard that at one farm the clock had been so far advanced that the sun did not rise till afternoon.

Iceland is full of the most delightful contrasts. While I sat waiting for the car, I brooded over the grimness of this country and its boundless solitudes, and the rain and hail fell, mingled with snow. Then the car came and it was full of the most beautiful young men, the driver, in particular, had exquisite eyelashes. The young men (three Icelanders and a Faroese) were all slightly tipsy and in the highest spirits, sipping whisky out of a little bottle, offering me cigarettes and talking what they called English. They insisted on my getting out of the car in the pouring rain and taking a photograph of them as they leant in carefully negligent attitudes against the side. They sang what they assured me were native melodies though one of them was curiously like "Ramona", and we bumped and skidded across the damp plain while the mountains frowned on us with disapproval.

Then I was back at the Hotel Godafoss with running water and electric light and a prospect of a hot bath in the morning.

The next fortnight I idled in Akureyri. The hotel was so comfortable, the streets and shops seemed so gay after the bleak hill-sides. Summer came, and in a night the country took on a new aspect. The fine grass, which is so sweet to taste that I was always nibbling it like a sheep, seemed to spring as you watched it. Vadlaheidi, across the fjord, had a new patch of green each day, where the grass and moss were clothing the bare rock. The streaks of white, hanging on its terraced side like threads of cotton seemed to thicken, as the snow melted and swelled the little waterfalls. The birches in the public gardens scented the genial air. I used to walk along the hill behind the town every evening till I came suddenly to a view of the fjord. There it lay, gently rippling in the breeze, while at the head the snow mountains reflected the sunset pinks. Here, up on the hillside, is the little cemetery of Akureyri, a desolate place of uncut grass, where the dead sleep in peace among the wistful wild-flowers.

They began to cut the hay and the hillsides were dotted with little patches of vivid green, which marked the day's work and the new mown field. Girls, their heads bound in coloured handkerchiefs, raked the new cut hay, moving with the rhythm and precision of a country dance. The scent of the hay drowned the fragrance of the birches. In the gardens along Hafnarstræti, the flowers bloomed.

There were so many things to watch — the boys leading in the hay, which was slung in two huge bundles, one on each side of a pony's back, the eider duck swimming with their young families in the fjord and seemingly confusing the babies so that one mother went home with the other's children, the fishermen pulling in the nets, while a group of delighted children pretended to help and actually hindered by throwing all the big fish back into the fjord and saving the tinies that should have been put back to grow up.

One day I stumbled on the *fjárrjett* (sheepfold), used when the sheep are driven down from the mountains for the shearing. There is a communal pen in a hollow about a mile from the town near the river Glerá. I was sitting there one morning in the sun, when I realised that there was a great deal of activity in this usually quiet place. People were gathering from all directions, from the hillside farms, but mostly from Akureyri. They were coming by foot, on horseback, on bicycles, by car,

by taxi. Then some of the horsemen rode off up the
mountain-side. In half an hour or so a thin trail of sheep
appeared. Soon the mountain-side was alive with sheep
and the air full of their distressed bleatings. After a
great deal of shouting and of barking from the dogs, the
sheep were safely driven down and penned in the big
central pen. Here the owners were walking up and down,
peering at the sheep, which kept up a constant hum of
protest at having been wrenched from the sweet mountain
grass. I was reminded of one of those awful drawing-
room games where you have to find someone with a
label corresponding to your own, so you walk round peering blindly, intent on labels. When the owner recognised
one of his own sheep, he carried it under his arm, if it was
a lamb, or put it between his legs if it was a ewe or a young
ram. Then he forced it into one of the smaller private
pens which radiate off from the central one. Here the
shearing took place. He, or she (for quite young girls
were doing it) inserted the shears (usually rusty old
scissors) and made a little cut at the top. Then the wool
was gently persuaded or peeled off, falling in an entire
mat, rather like the skin from a banana, while the clean
naked sheep emerged, like the freshly peeled fruit. The
belly was then carefully clipped and, if necessary, the
wool cut from the legs. Everyone was enjoying it, except
the sheep. The children played around and ate cake from
the paper bags of the Co-operative. Dogs barked and
were tiresomely officious. A group of ponies grazed
nearby.

Among the spectators from Akureyri was a Salvation
Army official whom I had met before in the boat. The
Army till a year or two ago was recruited and organised
from Denmark. But the Danes are not popular in Iceland,
and now the officers are from England or Scotland. I
met several of these exiles. They have a thankless piece
of work before them if they hope to convert the Icelanders
to the emotionalism of the Army. The girl I met watching

the sheep was a Scot and had been for some time in the Faroe Islands. She preferred the Faroese, finding them warmer-hearted than the Icelanders. She admitted that the manners of the Icelander were charming, but thought that beneath he was cold and critical. Incidentally she was engaged to one, so had every opportunity of knowing. But I suspect that as an official with the Salvation Army she would find the critical side of the Icelanders rather prominent, for all those I talked to considered the Army rather absurd. And so it seems in a country where there is little vice and little real destitution.

Quite innocently I made a gaffe with the Captain. She talked of a Chinese priest who had just come to Akureyri, who could speak Norwegian and Icelandic and who had been a missionary in five countries. So, pleased with the bizarrity, I said: "How interesting. He's come to convert the Icelanders to Confucianism." Then I realized he was an official in the Salvation Army.[20]

There are two picture theatres in Akureyri, but only one was open that summer. I saw some nice old-fashioned silent films, German and American, and was glad there were no talkies.

I went to a play one night. The company, who had produced the play in Reykjavik and had, I suppose, an amateur standing, were staying at the Godafoss, and it was interesting to watch the leading ladies charming the local shop-owners with their airs and graces. The play, "Hallsteinn and Dora", is by Einar Kvaran, one of the most distinguished prose writers alive in Iceland.[21] He has written charming stories but his later work has been rather spoilt by his habit of preaching Spiritualism. This play deals with that subject and is written mainly with the last act in view, an after-death scene. Hallstein, the hero, is an unpleasant character, selfish

---

[20] The "Chinese" priest could only have been the Icelander Ólafur Ólafsson who was a missionary in China for 14 years.
[21] Einar Kvaran (1859–1938).

and miserly. In the first act he and Dora get engaged. In the second they have a baby, which she produces in an incredibly short time while she is absent from the stage and he is discussing a new marriage with a rich widow. Then he insists on carrying his wife, in her childbed, out into the *baðstofa*, where she can be observed by the audience as she dies. In the third act he is about to hit the child, who is now a boy, but Dora appears in a white nightdress and the shock is so great that he dies. In the last act they are in *Ewigkeit*, which he mistakes for Thingvellir. He is in his ordinary suit, she in the white nightdress. They talk a good deal, and he becomes convinced that he is dead when a little curtain slides up at the back to show the hosts of the dead, all in white nightdresses, looking like a meeting of Romans in togas or an over-crowded Turkish bath. Finally she shows him that her love can outlast death, and the little curtain at the back slides up to reveal pink mountains with some palm trees, and they go off "to her mountain".

Outside the setting sun was painting a fantastic scene, much more unreal than that of the play.

I hired a bicycle or "wheel-horse" and tried to ride up and down the fjord. It was hard work and I should not recommend the bicycle as a means of transport. The roads are made of shingle roughly shovelled on to a bed of peat and rocks. Often the surface is less refined than shingle and shows large boulders. The surface is not rolled. That is left to the wheels of the passing cars so that the bicyclist is forced to keep in one or other of the wheel tracks of the cars. My hired bicycle was rather low so that the pedals were constantly catching in the sides of the ruts. I must have presented a pleasing picture to the Akureyrians as I laboured along in breeches with a large rucksack on my back containing books, a pump, and buns from the Co-op.

Still I got to the home of Gudmund the Powerful at Modruvellir, where he kept a thousand cows and a thousand sheep on what appeared to me insufficient grazing ground.[22] There also, up the valley, I reached the little church of Saurbær,[23] one of the few turf and timber churches left in Iceland. These old churches have been replaced by gay structures of wood or corrugated iron like the fine building at Grund which I passed on my way up the dale. I went also to the other Modruvellir down the fjord, where there was once an Augustinian monastery.[24]

After some days in Akureyri I began to feel that I could bear the great open spaces again, so I made plans for a tour to the east coast. My plans got as far as asking the price of a guide and horses, and finding it beyond my resources. The guide and the minimum possible of five horses would have cost about two pounds a day. So I decided to go by car as far as I could, i.e. to Myvatn, and then to hire a horse and guide from farm to farm, trusting as I neared the east coast to strike a motor road and then to walk or get lifts in cars. I also realised that it would be much cheaper to take a boat back from the east coast to Akureyri.

So on the twentieth of July I started in a car for Myvatn. There were the usual Icelandic false alarms about starting. Never during my stay did I find an expedition that started at the scheduled hour. This time it was to be at 6 a.m., so I packed in a panic. Then a message came to the hotel that it was to be seven. Then the time was altered to eight. So when we actually did start at 9.30 I had been up and waiting a good time. I had reduced my luggage to as little as possible and had only a rucksack and a *hnakktaska* or neat little canvas saddle-bag. I wore breeches and rubber boots, which I found essential, though uncomfortable, as we often had to

---

[22] *Sǫrla þáttr* is more modest in its claims for Guðmundr, to whom it assigns "hundrað hjóna ok hundrað kúa".
[23] Saurbær: this church was built by Séra Einar Thorlacius in 1858.
[24] The Augustinian monastery at Möðruvellir in Hörgárdalur was founded in 1296.

ride through rivers which came half way up my legs. Occasionally the water came higher and then I had the uncomfortable experience of riding with my boots full of water. I remember once emptying a quart out to the astonishment and amusement of my guide. I had no oilskins as I decided that they were too heavy to carry round and I trusted to an old Burberry for protection against the rain. The party in the car was a gay one and in holiday mood. It consisted of a young photographer who was combining business with pleasure. He had a very pretty and a very new wife with him. There was also a charming young man from the bicycle shop, whom I knew already as he had mended several punctures on my wheel-horse. Then there was his brother who owned and drove the car. They were off for a fishing expedition in the river Laxá and so also combining business with pleasure.

The journey was taken in holiday spirit. We made little detours to look at the view, to take photographs and to call on friends, as we did at Laugar in Ljosavatnsskard, where there is a fine school with a nice hot swimming bath. We ate sweets, smoked and had to unpack ourselves and the luggage while the car went through Ljosavatn, which had washed away the road so that cars are up to the axle in the lake. The ride was lovely, beginning with a long steep climb along the side of Eyjafjord from where we had a bird's eye view of Akureyri. Then we descended to Háls, which stands at the crossing of Ljosavatnsskard and Fnjoskadale. Here the steep banks of the ravine are covered with birch trees. Then we went along to Ljosavatn where, as I said before, we had to wait while the car swam the lake. Then a few miles on we reached the famous waterfall, Godafoss, had a lunch of milk, *skyr*, and cold meats, and walked along to admire the fall. It is a nice one, not nearly as terrifying as some I have seen. It doesn't fall from a great height but is very broad.

Then the road got worse and we crawled along cart-tracks, more rut than track, through the bleakest and dreariest country — lava with faint-hearted grass and flowers, and occasionally portentous rocks, looking like large solitary women brooding over their sorrows.

We jolted along what was less than a track and at last saw an expanse of grey-blue water with islands and fantastic black rocks. It was Myvatn. We lost it again, crossed Laxá where a colony of telephone workers were living in white tents, and arrived at Skutustadir at the head of the lake.

Myvatn, which means Mosquito Water, is one of the famous beauty spots in Iceland. It is certainly remarkable, lying as it does in a desert of lava. In the sunlight the colours must be marvellous, and even when I was there and the clouds were louring there was a sort of inky intensity about the land and water that was most impressive. The detail of this sinister landscape is surprisingly pretty. Here, as at Thingvellir, you find clefts in the lava full of exquisite flowers and grasses.

My heart sank a little as I stood there and looked down the lake. A bitter wind was blowing, which in one way was a blessing because it kept the mosquitoes away. A kind lady in Akureyri had lent me a green mosquito veil, but I didn't need to wear it more than once, and then only momentarily as we waited for the car to cross Ljosavatn. That was when I saw the sun for the last time for several days.

The farmhouse of Skutustadir was one of the old wooden ones and a curious old man with long hair was standing in the doorway. There was a church and the priest's house, which was a new and over-respectable structure. I stood and hesitated while the luggage was being unpacked from the car. I paid the driver, the car crawled off, and I felt that my last link with the west was gone. Then the photographer and his wife asked for coffee at the farm and I joined them. The hot drink gave me courage and, in spite of the photographer who pressed a wretched motor-boat on me, I said firmly to the lady of the house that I wanted a horse.[25] I added that it must be a very "quiet" one. I felt that the critical moment had come and if I did not mount a horse that evening I should never get my tour done. The lady of the house seemed to think that it was quite natural to want a horse, and with a good deal of miming (we both straddled on the chairs to show what sort of saddle I wanted, for at the time I was uncertain of the difference between *söðull* and *hnakkur*) we settled the matter between us.[26] Then she took me to see the church, which is gaily painted and has a chancel arch which simulates a rainbow — a pretty idea, I thought, in a country where the continuous rain might well drive one to despair.

Then my horse came, a "quiet" one, and mounting rather timidly I was off with the old man, whose hair streamed behind him like a comet's tail.

I enjoyed that reckless ride in the cold grey evening. The rocks were fantastic, the lava forming all sorts of ridiculous shapes. The distant mountains stood grimly by, the lake lay steely-grey to our left, and occasionally from the glassy surface a strange island reared itself, the crater of some small extinct volcano on the lake-bed. To our left was one mountain of black stuff that made me feel I was at home among the slagheaps of the Midland coal-fields. There were a great many funny little volcanic craters, like toy volcanoes.

The ends of the lake, Skutustadir and Reykjahlid, where I was to spend the night, were less grim. The lava is not so evident, and the hills and fields slope gently down to the water, as to any self-respecting lake.

At Reykjahlid I paid the old man the eight *krónur* that he asked. He said he had contemplated asking ten,

[25] There were two farms at Skútustaðir at this time. The lady of the house referred to was probably Árnína Soffía Jónsdóttir, the wife of the farmer Kristján Helgason.
[26] *Söðull* is a lady's side-saddle.

but that we had come so quickly that he would let me off the extra two. I thought that the estimate of four hours that they had suggested for the ride was a little excessive, as we had taken only two.

At Reykjahlid the farm-house is positively manorial.[27] They have thirty people working and living there. There are a father and mother and seven children, their wives, husbands and offspring and the hired people. The place is a regular halt on the west-east route and they seem to put up any number of guests at any time of the day or night. When I arrived without warning at ten o'clock on that summer evening I was given a delicious supper of flat bread, which is nice, brown and soft and cooked on a griddle, trout from the lake with melted butter, milk, rhubarb, porridge and cream. It was all very welcome after my cold ride. The food and general arrangements of the house are admirable.

Next morning I wandered about and looked at the church, which stands on a little island in the lava. When the red-hot lava swept down and devastated the region, the stream forked as it approached the church and left it untouched though the rest of the district was submerged.[28] While I poked around, the people of the house made arrangements for me and rang up my next stopping place, Grimsstadir. I was to be met at the river Jokulsá, ferried across and was to take another horse on the far side. I was accompanied by a *fylgðarkona*, a woman guide, a grave, spectacled daughter of the house who was to accompany me on the five-hour ride through one of the most desolate districts in Iceland, a lava waste, where we were to see no sign of life for the whole five hours, unless the sheep from Grimsstadir could be counted as such.

---

[27] There were no less than four farmers in Reykjahlíð, so that it is impossible to say for certain to whom Miss Selby applied for lodging.
[28] This eruption, known as Mývatnseldar (1724–29), destroyed the farm at Reykjahlíð but spared the church. An account of the eruption was written by the priest Jón Sæmundsson and printed in Copenhagen in 1726.

A journey to the East

This part of Iceland borders the great desert of Odádahraun ("the lava of ill-deeds"). It stretches inland to the mountains Herdubreid and Askja and to the great glacier, Vatnajokul, which comes down almost sheer to the south coast. It is a place of ill association for outlaws used to take refuge there. Here also the trolls and creatures of ill-omen were supposed to live and breed. And here are volcanoes which are not yet extinct and craters with the potentialities of ruin. It is indeed a grim land.

I mounted my horse with care for I was suffering from the reckless riding of the night before, and we set out towards the peculiar red hills I had seen in the east and which I had thought were flooded with sunshine, while all the rest of the countryside was clouded. But as we drew near I found that it was their natural colour; they were the Námafjall (the mountain of the mines), so called because they are potential sulphur and brimstone mines. Smoke curls constantly from the red and yellow ground. We soon passed the mines and came into a belt of vegetation — low scrub, bilberries and the like. Then followed devastating stretches of lava and black soil, with only rare patches of coarse green grass. It seemed as if it would never end; the telegraph posts marched on, a slender army of civilization, and our horses' hoofs continued to beat up the black dust. The way was marked by cairns, one every hundred yards or so. I was glad of them, for when we had been riding for a few hours my guide cheerfully told me that she had never been to Jokulsá before, and I did not like the picture of two horse-women lost in the wastes of the great desert. The last hour seemed a long one and the distant mountains drew no nearer. I noticed one peculiarity, that the soil was always damp, through an inch or two of black dust. I believe that this is due to the melting snow from the distant mountains. Then, quite suddenly, we saw a white hut and came to the bank of the river which washes

its swift way through low sides of black soil. It is a
desolate place with the stones bleaching on its dark banks
like the skulls of famine-stricken sheep.

    The *bóndi* from Grimsstadir was waiting with the ferry
boat and on the other side of the river two horses were
grazing. I said good-bye to my guide and gave her a
piece of chocolate to cheer her on her solitary ride home.
We rowed across the swift river and pulled the boat up
above the high-water mark. I climbed painfully onto a
grey, and it dashed away as if it was Tom Mix's horse
Tony. I clung on desperately for the four kilometres
from the river and prayed that I should not fall off.
Miraculously I didn't, despite the rucksack swaying
dangerously behind me.

    Then came one of the most acceptable coffees of my
life in the nice upstairs front room of Grimsstadir. The
family were very friendly and gathered in the parlour
to talk to me.[29] There were two nice boys, a large kind
mother and a lovely little blonde girl from Akureyri who
was spending her holidays there. She was a brilliant
teacher of her own language and I was glad to practise
my Icelandic. I found everywhere in Iceland that I
could learn better from children than grown-ups; they
talked so distinctly and were so sympathetic and amused.
I had a pot of very strong tea with my supper — a kind
thought on the part of the *bóndi*'s wife who knew that the
English drank tea. After supper I went on a walk across
the blank country, which is growing with grass and two
kinds of willow scrub, one green and one silvery leaved.
I was guided on my walk by a black and white dog and
the smallest black and white goat that I had ever seen;
it was two weeks old and accompanied me with the
same fidelity as the dog. It was nice to feel that in these
wastes there were two creatures that could understand
me when I spoke. Goats, by the way, are common in

---

[29] There were three farmers at this time at Grímsstaðir. Probably the family referred to was that of Ingólfur Kristjánsson and Katrín Magnúsdóttir.

this part of Iceland though they are not generally seen elsewhere.

I discovered that Grimsstadir is not as isolated as I thought. It has a motor road leading to Axarfjord, where there is a trading station. The road is imperceptible, and the telegraph lines stretch grimly on to the east, pointing the way I had to go.

Next morning I sat looking out of my window and waiting to start. The sky was still dull, and under the louring clouds lay a featureless landscape, flat for miles, with the distant mountains an inky blue. The most obvious vegetation is the cotton grass which brightens the dull green with its white tufts. I was waiting for a man who was going to Modrudale, and taking what I understood, with my imperfect Icelandic, to be a parcel. I found that I was getting used to being handed on from farm to farm and felt quite passive, as if I was a parcel myself.

The "parcel" arrived about one and proved to be a train of a dozen pack-ponies and two riding ponies, one of which was to be mine. The pack-ponies were carrying unwieldy loads — two sacks of flour, with a few supernumerary bags, three large wooden boxes, some scythe handles and hay rakes, and an agricultural machine of some sort. My own luggage was tied on top of one of the burdens and only fell off once, when I unpicked my camera from it and trusted that my toothbrush wouldn't drop out. We started soon after one, and I was rather dashed, after a few hours riding, when a young man told me that we shouldn't be at Modrudale till ten that evening. However, it turned out that he was speaking in terms of "country time", which was two or three hours ahead of the "telephone time".

It was very cold and the sand was blowing thickly in some places. The poor ponies carrying the heaviest loads lay down every few minutes and tried to rub the wooden boxes off their backs. The string with which the various objects were tied on came undone, and the ponies had to be calmed from their fright. The young man treated them with patience and consideration and did not allow himself to be annoyed, even when his own horse galloped off while he was attending to one of the pack-animals and he had to chase after it on foot and coax it back.

We made our way across the desert, yellow sand and black sand, patches of bent grass and dried-out river beds, sometimes full of snow-water. The farther mountains were shrouded, the nearer ones black, purple and sometimes red, but always ominous. The monotony seemed intolerable. Then we climbed a little col and came down to another expanse of desert with the blue mountains still far off. There was a flicker of sunshine and the black flats shimmered. Then more desert, and then the green began, *mýri* or swamp grass, and a *bær* in the valley — Vididale.[30] We stopped and my young man untied some of the bundles and retied them. Some children came out with wool, and a sad-faced young woman came quietly out and talked in an unenthusiastic way. We were soon off again through the quickly diminishing green into the desert. We climbed another col, with some jagged rocks this time to break the monotony, and came down a curious little pass to a river and the plain. More desert, more *mýri*, then in the distance an object which proved to be Modrudale. We had ridden thirty-five kilometres and taken seven hours.

There I found a party of two English ladies and two Americans, who were riding with twenty horses and four guides. The English ladies, characteristically enough, had gone to bed, the Americans, equally characteristically, were sitting up to inspect the English woman, whose coming had been flashed ahead over the telephone wires. Our ways crossed for that night only, as they

---

[30] Víðidalur was then farmed by Þorsteinn Jóhannes Sigurðsson and Guðrún Sigurbjörnsdóttir.

were returning to Akureyri and I was going east. But later we happened on each other a good deal, in several unexpected places. I was very grateful for their existence, partly because in many of the farms where I stayed the caravan provided a topic of conversation and partly because the contrast in our way of travelling impressed the farmers with the others' riches as opposed to my poverty, and as a result they were moderate in their charges to me.

The next day was uncompromisingly wet, not with mere *þoka* or mist of which I had already seen so much, but with a real downpour. The Anglo-American caravan started at ten, the ladies all rather green and dispirited, the guides worried because three of their ponies were missing and one had lamed itself on some barbed wire. The *bóndi* suggested I should wait until next day, and as I was incompletely equipped for heavy rain, I was glad to accept his invitation. So we watched the ladies off and turned back into the house to a sort of ghost coffee-party — ten cups, saucers, plates, a large coffee-pot and two huge cream cakes, all laid for the departed ladies and their guides. The *bóndi* and I sat and nibbled the fringes of this banquet.

Rain all day. The missing ponies are not found. A guide has been left behind to look for them, and he drops into the best room and drinks an occasional cup of coffee. The married daughter sits and talks to me, and I am quickly improving my Icelandic. It's a self-contained group at Modrudale, father, mother, three sons, two daughters, the husband of one of them, and the ensuing children.[31] There are no workmen or workwomen, and they live in this isolation with their eight cows, forty horses and three or four hundred sheep. I suppose they are quite wealthy; they make a little money from the visitors who stop the night, but it cannot be much as they charge so little.

[31] According to the 1930 census the farmer at Möðrudalur was Jón Aðalsteinn Stefánsson and his wife Þórunn Vilhjálmsdóttir.

It is a long day on that lonely farm, and I sit and read the hymn book and learn by heart the Icelandic version of "Onward, Christian soldiers". The rain drips steadily on the zinc roof. The windows of the *stofa* are steamed over. Then I moved to the *frammistofa*, my bedroom. It's cold and the door doesn't shut properly. They've been washing the floors and there is no carpet. A bowl of cold water on the table awaits my toilet. Outside the brown-green of the *tún* stretches down to a little river. Beyond that is the lava plain, ringed round by those sinister mountains. I have read the hymn book. I have read my Icelandic grammar, and now I go to bed to learn the adjective by heart and hope I sleep. The lost horses have not been found.

The next day was even wetter, and the *þoka* thicker. I decided to stay. The day drifted by. I read a novel by Hulda,[32] whose characters always die. I re-read the hymn-book, and my grammar. I ate, went for a walk in the rain, ate again, read, and was thinking of going to bed, when I saw a little boy driving the cows home. So I went and practised my Icelandic grammar on him in the cowshed, which was by far the dryest and warmest place, as my bedroom roof had now begun to leak. Then I walked down with my nice Johanna, the married daughter, and a small girl to milk the goats. In the *tún* they were cutting the grass. Whilst we were busy with the goats, the little girl, who was standing on the roof of the *fjós*, called out that horses were coming, and we saw an army galloping towards us. We saw two men riding up and decided it was guests. We all got excited and carried the milk back to the farm, where the sons of the house, with admirable self-control, were continuing their mowing. But they too were tempted to come, and there was great excitement when the army of ponies rode up and were safely corralled in the *rétt*.

---

[32] Hulda was the pseudonym of Unnur Benediktsdóttir Bjarklind (1881–1946).

Then the two drovers got off their horses and with the utmost politeness said good-evening to everyone, shaking hands all round and murmuring their names. Then there was a conversation about the ultimate destination of the ponies, which were being driven east over Jokulsá to be sold. After that we had coffee in the best room, my host, the two men and I, and we talked personalities mostly — the Anglo-American caravan, me, and other visitors. The men, like most Icelandic men, have low, husky voices. Some of the women have soft voices too, but some have peculiarly strident ones. But it's a lesson in good manners to hear these country folk say "Gerið svo vel" as they hand you the sugar and to see the quiet way in which they rise at the end of the meal and shake hands with the host, saying "Thank you for the meal".

Next day was less wet, though one could hardly count it fine. Still we decided it was good enough to start in; so we set off at one. With me was a daughter of the house and a tiny girl who is some sort of adoptee, a pack-pony, and the two horse-drovers and their thirty or forty untamed animals. We were making for Eiriksstadir, a farm on the river Jokulsá. The girls intended to combine the business of guiding me with the pleasure of staying there a few days, as the *bóndi* at Eiriksstadir was an uncle or related in some way to the Modrudalers. It was a nice ride, diversified by wild-west incidents when the ponies strayed from the track. The desert was slightly more varied, at least there were ups and downs and the sun occasionally shone. We climbed a pass and came down to a green dale with a lake and swans flying over it. At the end of the lake there was a farm where we had coffee.[33] I was glad to see it as it was the first of the tiny turf houses I had been inside. It was like going into a fortress through the elaborate turf passages.

[33] This farm must have been Sænautasel, a small farm which was abandoned in 1942. The farmer was Guðmundur Guðmundsson and the housekeeper Halldóra Eiríksdóttir.

Then we came into the kitchen which had been beautifully scrubbed for Saturday — it was *laugardagur*. There was a stove with peat and *tað*, a table, a quantity of chests and boxes of white wood, from which cakes and biscuits were produced. There was also a pretty painted chest of drawers, a bride's chest I assumed. A ladder staircase led to the bedroom and there was one window which looked out at the level of the ground, because the house is built below ground level. We sat in the neat sparse kitchen while the Modrudale daughter fiddled with a pan of water at the stove, rather vaguely making coffee. The *húsfreyja* got out the best cups, dusted them, and wiped them with a drop of water from the coffee pan. The biscuits and sponge-cakes were produced and we ate and drank, at first shyly, and talked in subdued whispers. But as the coffee got into our systems, we became gayer, and the hostess and her guests were soon laughing and chattering quite nicely. I've noticed that the people on the isolated farms don't know what to do in the first minutes of meeting a visitor. They are ill at ease; it's almost as though they resent the violation of their solitude, but quite soon — and especially if they sit at coffee — they become pleased at the human contact and seem sorry to be left alone.

This woman lived alone with her husband and her children. The eldest child was a boy of about fifteen. Her husband was away, taking his wool to the nearest Co-operative store, a two-day's journey off in Vopnafjord. She was with child. When her time came the midwife would ride to tend her, and perhaps one of the women from Modrudale or Eiriksstadir would cross the twenty kilometres of desert that separates the farms and stay for a few days to look after the children. When anyone in these isolated farms is very ill, they are taken into hospital on a sort of bier which is fastened between two horses, and so for perhaps two days they are jolted over the mountains and across the rivers.

A journey to the East

We rode away in the chill of the evening. Dark clouds came up and we lost the track. We passed another tiny farm,[34] lying at the side of a little lake in a little green dale. We asked the way, found the track, lost it again. Then we scrambled round the side of Eiriksstadir Hnefill, a little knobbly mountain, and on and on, till we came out suddenly on a steep, green hillside, with a green hill opposite, which — though I was not aware of it at first — was on the other side of Jokulsá. The track turned down and far below us we saw the tiny church of Eiriksstadir.

The herd of horses hurried down the steep track, scrambling, slipping, biting each other in the excitement of realising that they were getting near their night's rest. We followed more sedately on our tired horses and waited outside the *tún*, while warning was given of our arrival. There was a faint drizzle, and as I stood looking round everything seemed bright green after the dreary lava wastes — the cut hay on the *tún*, the turf walls, the turf roof of the out-houses, and the hillside across the river.

We arrived about ten, but it was after one when we got to bed, having eaten two meals — the inevitable coffee which is served as a sort of cocktail and then a supper of cold meats and *skyr*. It was the first dark evening of the summer; the hill across the river keeps the light away and there was a grey sky. We ate our meals in the twilight dusk of the front room, so that it was by faith that one speared a piece of smoked meat or made advances to the butter, and one's conversation was addressed to a grey, faceless shadow across the table.

The *bóndi* at Eiriksstadir was charming, spectacled and grey-haired. He plays the organ. Most of the farms in Iceland have an American organ. This instrument has ousted the old-time fiddle or zither. He was like Tom Pinch, vague, sweet-natured and musical, and had the sprouting hair that one sees in Cruikshank's

[34] Veturhús which was abandoned in 1941.

interpretation of that character.[35] I had a charming picture of him in the morning, sitting in a sort of storeroom where the harmonium was housed with tools and sheeps' fleeces littering the bare boards. He was playing the organ and surrounded by a group of flaxen-haired children, his own little short-sighted son at his side peering at the music. They were singing national melodies in the shrill tuneless way that is common to the children of all nations.

Next day was Sunday and my host pressed me to stay and rest. I was not very keen to do this because I saw that I would have to hurry if, as I intended, I was to cross the river to Hrafnkelsdale, and then get to Seydisfjord in time to catch the boat back to Akureyri. But partly because I realised that none of them wanted to turn out on Sunday to guide me down the dale, partly because they were so nice that I was glad to spend a day with them, I accepted the invitation. Mother was away, she had taken one of the little girls to Seydisfjord to get spectacles, and the house was being run by two nieces, aged fourteen and sixteen. They were not very competent about the house, so coffee did not come to my bedside till eleven o'clock. Then I dressed and went out, and found a very Sunday group of men lazing out in the sun before the house. There was no service in the little church that day. The country pastors have often four or five churches in their care, so that each church gets a service only once a month or so.

I had hoped to cross Jokulsá at Eiriksstadir and so reach Hrafnkelsdale, which lies a little further up on the other side. I found that the "bridge" there was merely a suspended basket running on wires across the swift, deep river. I wished to cross in this but my host said that it was quite impossible and very dangerous for a

[35] There were two farmers at Eiríksstaðir. The one referred to here was Jón Gunnlaugsson Snædal and his wife was Stefanía Katrín Karlsdóttir. I have been unable to find a Cruikshank drawing of Tom Pinch. Perhaps the illustration of *Martin Chuzzlewit* by Phiz was meant.

woman, and the basket was only for inanimate objects and the most level-headed men. As he refused to operate it and as it was impossible to work it by myself, I was forced to give up the idea of seeing Hrafnkelsdale. So after lunch I took a walk up the dale to see, like Moses from Pisgah, my promised dale afar off. It was very hot near the river and the flies were troublesome, so I climbed the mountain and had a bird's eye view of my dale. I got back to Eiriksstadir about seven. The farm was deserted, the horses and their drovers had gone, and with them most of the family. The children and the girls were busy at the back of the house. I sat on the front step and felt as if it was a Sunday evening of my childhood, when the family had all gone to church and left me behind to take care of the house. It was very quiet in the dale. About nine the first of the wanderers returned, and at ten we sat down to supper.

Monday was wet. All night the rain had been beating on the roof, and there was a rhythmical tapping in the corner of my room, where the rain was steadily dropping into my wash basin. The roofs of all these farms were leaking just now, because they had just had a dry spell and the wood had shrunk. With continued rain the wood would swell, and the leaking season pass. I was glad to think so, for the sake of those poor people in the winter rains and snows.

The family was disorganised. Mother and a crowd of children had come back late at night while I was asleep, and still later a man arrived with parcels from the east. So morning coffee came at twelve, and it was after two when we sat down to lunch. It was decided that I should go on to a farm down the dale, where there was a proper bridge and spend the night there.[36]

I was accompanied by the Modrudale girls and a bright

---

[36] Before the construction of the bridge at Fossvellir which was capable of taking a motor car, there was a rather frail bridge at Hákonarstaðir where the old bridle-path crossed Jökulsá.

little boy who had been staying at Eiriksstadir and was returning, as far as I could understand, to Seydisfjord. He was very small and looked about eight. He had a genius both for understanding my imperfect Icelandic and making me understand his, so the adults in the house used to turn to him to interpret their conversation. It was partly that he spoke slowly and distinctly, and partly that he had a great gift for synonyms and definitions. He was also as kind as he was clever and insisted on lending me his lovely little horse, Baldur, which was one of the smoothest moving horses I rode. Our little party started about four and he guided us very competently down the dale, though the mist was so thick that we could hardly see the track. We stopped once for coffee, as the little boy insisted on calling on some friends. It was almost ten when we reached Hakonarstadir,[37] and there the children drank more coffee, though I could see that the eldest girl was worrying at the lateness of the hour and the fact that they all had a long way to go. But my boy-friend insisted in a lordly way on the coffee and on inspecting the cattle-sheds. Then they rode off through the mist, this party of children hardly out of the nursery, and I was left alone at Hakonarstadir.

It was a grim place, the only really unpleasant house that I stayed in when I was in Iceland. To begin with, I was rather shaken by meeting a bull, which was straying loose round the house, and as I had been unnerved by a previous encounter with a bull calf, I didn't feel too friendly towards it. But an old man with a pitchfork drove it in. Then the housewife was discontented, grumbling to me about the desolation of the district and how she missed the gaiety of Vopnafjord. The husband was sinister, the old farm-hand an unprepossessing figure with a week-old beard and bleary eyes. There were three pasty little boys who played rude games outside my

---

[37] According to the 1930 census, Hákonarstaðir was farmed by Sigvaldi Jónsson and his wife Jónína Rustikusdóttir.

window. The house was dirty, the floor black, the walls of my room painted with age-old yellow paint, which was peeling with leprous patches. Then it thundered and lightened and the rain came down in torrents.

Next day the aspect was hardly less sinister, and there was trouble about the horses which couldn't be found. I sat for three hours in the unclean parlour looking out at the dark hill which seemed too near and which shut out the light from the valley. Indeed, this particular bit of Jokuldale is shut in on all sides by high green hills, and there is no distant prospect of the mountains as in so many Icelandic valleys. As I sat there and looked out through the dirty Nottingham lace curtains, I felt as if I were in a trap and should never get out of Jokuldale, and still less to Hallormsstad, Seydisfjord, Akureyri, Reykjavik, Leith and London.

The horses were found at last and we were ready to leave. Then the postman came on his fortnightly call — he leaves the letters as he goes up the dale, and calls for the replies as he comes back. That meant another hour was spent in conversation.

My guide was rather disconcerting as he had one arm in a sling, but he proved to be a charming young man, friendly, gay and talkative. We crossed the river and climbed the steep side of the Fljotsdale Herad. Then we went across the top, a bleak expanse of land with a little grass and bilberry scrub, a great many rocks, much water and unmelted snow. We splashed and trotted over the heath, and chattered. My guide had been in hospital in Seydisfjord with five English sailors and "understood" English. How much, I didn't investigate. But he recited the names of the five sailors, asked me if I knew them and said that he had found them *gaman* (fun).

After two hours riding we came into *þoka* and stayed in it for the rest of the day, so that our spirits and our clothes were equally damped. At first it was impressive on that mountain top to see the brooks gleaming bleakly through the mist, and still more to see the sheen of what were apparently uphill-sloping lakes, only to find, as one drew close, that they were large banks of snow. We came down eventually into the mists of Fljotsdale. We passed a farm called Bessastadir to reach the ferry which was to carry me over Lagarfljot, a large lake that cuts the west off from the east coast. We galloped over some wet meadows, through a river, and across some even wetter meadows, to come out on the banks of a large white expanse in which the water and the mist were hardly to be distinguished. We could just see a green strip opposite with a house. The young man took a deep breath, hollowed his hand, and called "fe-e-e-erja". There was a silence and then a faint echo of "fe-e-e-erja" mocked us from the hills and rolled round the lake. This happened several times, and in the silence between the calls and the echo we could hear nothing but the horses as they cropped the grass of the meadow. Then a thin childish voice called across the lake that the ferry was not at home, but would be back in two hours. I felt as if I should never see England again, but was doomed to spend my life suspended between west and east. So we galloped back to Bessastadir, and while I waited in the rain, my spirits at their lowest, the young man fetched the mistress of the house.[38] She was a tiny, straight-backed, rosy-cheeked old lady with two plaits of hair, a clean blue cotton frock, no teeth, but the pinkest little mouth and tongue. I waited in the parlour among a collection of books, English, Danish, German, Icelandic and in about half an hour the old lady came back with coffee. I was still feeling rather depressed, but was cheered by the hot coffee and the lace-like pancakes spread with jam. I congratulated her on them, and she giggled at my bad Icelandic. Then I made a remark about my gloves which were wet, but with my confused vocabulary I called them *kettlingur* (kitten) instead of

[38] Probably Anna Jóhannsdóttir.

vettlingar (gloves). The old lady became helpless with laughter, I giggled too, and we became the fastest of friends. She took me out in the rain into her garden, taught me the names of flowers, and picked me a little bunch of poppies, Baldur's Brow, crane's bill and a pungent herb that might be tansy. Then the young man came out to say that the two hours had elapsed. We said goodbye, and she asked me to write my name on a piece of paper, "because I was so nice that she wanted to remember my name". I gave her a visiting card and she was delighted. I had found that this was a simple way of giving pleasure to my hosts and hostesses in the country, and judging by the objects that already littered their best rooms I believe that my visiting cards would be treasured for years, and that future travellers will see them getting dustier and dustier among the miscellaneous objects on the what-not in remote country farms.

I felt much brighter as we galloped for the third time over the water-meadows, and I reflected how I had found so often in Iceland that the inhospitable landscape of this bleak country was cheered by some warm human contact. But even as I sniffed my fragrant nosegay on the banks of Lagarfljot I was to receive another rebuff. Again the cry of "fe-e-e-erja" rolled across the lake and again the echoes mocked us from the hills. I felt that Lagarfljot was another Jordan, and across it lay the promised land or at least the key to all the amenities of civilization, and that I was fated never to arrive. We stood for perhaps half an hour in the mist. The young man was concerned and determined in a spectacular sort of way, saying that he would get me across to Hrafnkelsstadir, come what might. But when we discussed alternatives to the ferry he had none to offer. It was too difficult to swim the horses across and there was no other ferry. So he showed his sympathy by turning to me very often and saying "Ekki kalt?" ("Not cold, are you?"). At last there was some sign of activity on the bank opposite, or at least the young man alleged that he could see the boat. I could see nothing through the mist, but soon the creak of oars came to my ears and the boat arrived. It was manned by two boys in blue dungarees. They had reddish hair and pink faces out of which the bluest eyes stared solemnly. And indeed they might well stare, for I must have been a curious figure looming out of the mist, in breeches and rubber boots with my rucksack on my back and a bunch of flowers in my hand.

We rowed slowly across the lake. Then came what might well have been the final catastrophe. About half way across the boat slowed even more, and the boys announced we had run aground. Now I could not help laughing, for the idea of spending the rest of my life actually on Lagarfljot, not merely ranging up and down Jokulsdale, seemed so funny. The boys laughed too and the catastrophe was not as serious as it had seemed. One of them climbed out of the boat and simply towed it ashore.

I had a nice night there at Hrafnkelsstadir. The new house is of concrete and seemed warm and dry. The roof didn't leak though the rain beat on it all night long. The walls were painted a nice bright blue. I had company in the upstairs room, a schoolmaster who was staying in the house and who came up with one of the blue-eyed boys, both of them obviously shaved and dressed in neat dark suits, collars and ties for the benefit of the English lady. They talked a great deal, asked questions about England, looked up places on a map; the schoolmaster corrected my pronunciation and genders and was patient and delightful. They seemed very gay after the rather grim household of Hakonarstadir.

Next day started well. One of the boys guided me to Hallormsstad. We had a pleasant ride and made a detour to look at the tallest tree in the wood there, a birch tree that was quite ten feet high. This corner of Lagarfljot is prettily covered with birch woods, which run down to the lake edge. We were making for Hallormsstad where there is a school of Domestic Economy for girls. I had heard about this school and that the building was a new one, and I intended to spend the night there, as I hoped to find at last the conveniences I had failed to find anywhere else on my tour. But because of my own ineptitude I was destined to spend the night in another damp bed and old-fashioned farmhouse. The mist had come down again, so that when we arrived at a house and were taken into the sitting-room I assumed that I was at the new school, though I must admit that I was disappointed as the house seemed no different from any other good-sized Icelandic farm. The host came in, welcomed me, we drank coffee, and I asked if I could stay the night. Then I found that I had planted myself on a timid embarrassed widower,[39] who was too hospitable to say "Why don't you stay at the school?", which was indeed not a hundred yards away though hidden by the mists. He was kind enough to make me welcome and next day to invite me, as it was still raining, to stay for the night and to inspect the school.

His sister is the schoolmistress.[40] She is fat, wears horn-rimmed spectacles and is of the universal type, which would be as convincing in a high-necked shirt blouse as the headmistress of an English High School as she was in national dress presiding over twenty Icelandic young ladies. I spent an interesting day with her. She speaks English well and has an assorted library, ranging from the Old Norse Sagas to Dean Inge and "Companionate Marriages". She is intensely nationalistic, and on winter evenings the girls gather round her with their spinning wheels and she reads the Old Icelandic poetry aloud to them, just as a cultured British schoolmistress might read Yeats to her pupils. We talked a

---

[39] Guttormur Pálsson. It is interesting to note that this shy, embarrassed widower married his second wife only a month after Miss Selby's visit.
[40] Sigrún Pálsdóttir Blöndal.

great deal about national integrity. Her girls worry her by wanting to wear silk underclothes and playing the gramophone; she thinks the Icelanders are becoming effete and have no pride in their history because they don't spin and weave their stockings from the wool of their own sheep. She disapproves of the Danish influences on food and the introduction of cakes and coffee, though she approves of the native pancake.

The building, in the creation of which she had a hand, is dominated by the *baðstofa*. The hand-work room has panelling and a sloping roof, and windows that are too small. Some of the bedrooms are also designed on that model, and the schoolmistress hopes to introduce *lokrekkjur*, the rather unhygienic cupboard-beds of the old farmhouses. She talked a good deal about the Icelander's lack of a furniture-sense. Her own room is very nice. One wall is filled with books, lovely old leather-bound editions of the sagas and geographies of Iceland. On the other walls are two or three paintings by modern Icelandic artists. There is a wide window with a picture better than any of the paintings, an exquisite view of Lagarfljot, with the mountains on the other side streaked with the white threads of falling torrents. I was a little contemptuous of the more practical side of this new building. The sanitary arrangements were hardly up-to-date; it is true there was a bathroom, but it was in the basement, was unventilated and smelt.

Next day was bright with sunshine. I said goodbye to my embarrassed host and set out free as the wind, because for the first time since leaving Akureyri I was travelling alone and on foot. I felt free and happy to dawdle along at my own pace and not the guide's or the horse's, to start when I liked, to stop when I liked, and even to take off my boots and paddle in the lake, though I had felt no temptation to do this earlier on the mist-shrouded mountains. The road went through the birch woods, which were no longer fragrant, as they had been in last night's rain. I had had particular experience of this fragrance the evening before when I had taken refuge in a thick coppice from a young bull, which had snorted and roared around my shelter for half an hour. At last it had tired and I slunk home. When I made an allusion to this terrifying animal, my host had said: "He's quite harmless. He only does that for fun." He certainly got his fun that night.

The road left the woods and ran along the shore of the lake for some miles. It was so hot I played with the idea of bathing, but I played too long for the road left the shore and turned inland for a mile or so. I stopped at a farm and asked for milk, and a pleasant woman, hot from hay-making, gave me a jug free and would take no payment. She showed me some old side-saddles, with seats of embroidered velvet and a little rail at the back. Then I tramped on in the sun and rested often, because my pack and rucksack were burdensome. Rather suddenly I came to Egilsstadir, a group of three or four concrete buildings standing at the edge of the Fljot which narrows here almost to the width of a broad river and is spanned by a long slender bridge. There was a nice green petrol pump at the side of the road, and I nearly threw my arms round it as I felt it was a messenger from the great civilized world of baths and tramcars.

At Egilsstadir there is an hotel. I had for the last few days been brooding over this and planning what I should have for supper when I got there. I was looking forward to being in a place where I could give orders as to my comfort, and not feel that I was being obtrusive or a nuisance as one is bound to be sometimes when one arrives at a private house as an uninvited guest. So I marched in and firmly ordered a hot supper. I was a little dashed when they said that it would be ready at eight-thirty; I suggested they should hurry it up a little as I was hungry. It came ten minutes before it was due.

I ordered a packet of cigarettes, and with an intense sense of luxury lit the last survivor of the last packet I had brought from Akureyri. I ordered a bottle of beer — poor stuff this, but the best one can hope for in a semi-prohibition country. Then I ordered breakfast for eight o'clock, with bread and butter and no cake. Finally I ordered a packet of sandwiches to be ready for me at nine. My orders were received with the utmost respect and I even thought of putting my shoes out to be cleaned, but I decided that perhaps that would be going a little far.

It was grey and misty as I went to bed, and from my large window, which did not open, I could see the white water of the lake and the grey hills. All the day the lake had been blue and the mountains quite distinct — Snæfell to the south and other snow-topped peaks to the north.

Egilsstadir is a beauty spot, famous I had been told for its trees. I didn't notice any. Breakfast, brought punctually at eight, was a curious but not unpalatable meal of coffee and bread and butter overlaid with meat and cheese. There was a dish of jam. I removed the meat, but grappled with the cheese which went very well with the jam. It was a nice morning with rather subdued sunshine. Snæfell was peering over the hills at the top of the lake.

I had a mountain to climb before I could reach Seydisfjord, so I left the motor road which I had followed since Hallormsstad. The climb up the mountain was hard; the sun shone and my two bags were heavy, but the view over Lagarfljot was superb. The snow was still lying on the mountain top and sometimes unnerving. I had long snow bridges to cross, and here and there were cracks in the snow revealing steep ravines filled with rushing torrents. Where the snow had melted was mud. This was even more unnerving as, though it was deceptively firm to the eye, one could easily sink down into it to the knee. I thought what a nasty death it would be to drown in thick mud. The mountain top was bleak and stoney, with very little vegetation and a few sheep nibbling what little there was. When I reached the flat top the river I had been following broadened out into an untidy lake, and I saw that a stream was running down the other side to Seydisfjord. One could just detect the ridge where the streams parted. There were a great many other lakes formed by springs and melting snow.

The path turned down and I entered a narrow, long, steep valley. Below, the river foamed and spread into blue and white patches. Far far away I could see a corner of the fjord and round it the tiny white houses of the village. It was a long time till I reached it, and I had a river to cross; the water got into my boots. As I went down I met a party on horseback, the first people I had seen since leaving Egilsstadir. Then I met more and more till there was a regular procession. I thought that it was the usual Saturday exodus from the towns, and felt that it was faintly like the Brighton road. I learned later that it was the August holiday and that the people from Seydisfjord always spent that weekend at Egilsstadir.

Seydisfjord looked a little dingy when I entered it. I had heard that there was an hotel in Seydisfjord, and further that this hotel was kept by an English woman. So I had pictured a nice, clean place like the one at Akureyri, made even more comfortable by its English proprietress. I thought I should arrive to find a nice clean room, a hot bath, a pot of tea, and a little sympathetic conversation. I was rather dashed to find that the hotel of which I had heard so much, and indeed the only hotel in Seydisfjord, was the Salvation Army Hostel. The English woman was there all right; but she was Scotch, and a pathetic anaemic Army Captain, who was so conscious of her exile that I got quite enough conversation to make up for all that I had missed in the past fortnight. The rooms were not clean, and though there was a bathroom, the furnace was broken and the water supply defective. However, my room had a lovely big balcony, and from it I could sit and watch the sun gilding the mountain tops.

It doesn't gild Seydisfjord, which is shut in by mountains on all sides. Even the mouth of the fjord is closed so that one cannot see the open sea. It must be a gloomy place in the dark winter days, but it was rather charming in the reflected autumn sunshine. The mountains near the town are so sheer that you feel that they may slip at any minute and bury the town. Indeed I was told that avalanches were an ever-present danger.

The town was gloomy that weekend because all the gay young people had gone over to Egilsstadir. But in any case there is a feeling of desolation about it; it has seen better days for it grew to its present size through the herring industry. Then, as a result of the mysterious and incalculable movement of the fish, the North coast and Siglufjord became the centre of the industry. Seydisfjord remains a monument to financial instability with only its bank and its three-storied houses to tell its former glories.

The boat was late so I had three days to wait. I found it interesting because I amassed a great deal of information about the Army, some of it rather discreditable. This young girl had been sent out like all the officers in foreign service with no fixed salary. She was given free quarters in the Hostel, which was run by an Icelandic woman, but for money she had to depend on what she could collect from the inhabitants (and that was very little as, like most Icelanders, they were contemptuous of the Army), and what she could wheedle out of the Norwegian and English sailors who called at the port. When a boat came in she went on board — if they would let her for Army officers, like clergymen, are considered to bring bad luck — and handed round her collecting box.

There was no one to keep any check on her accounts, so she had the opportunity of helping herself, an obvious stimulus to assiduous collecting. The Army, as far as I could see, served no useful purpose in Seydisfjord. There were no slums, no drunken wife-beaters to be converted, no destitute men to house and feed. The hostel was run purely as a commercial proposition and used by business men as an hotel. The Captain had succeeded in persuading six little girls to become girl guides, but as the little girls were Icelanders, they already had the qualities of resource, reliance and honesty that the Guide Movement is supposed to encourage. A meeting was held once a fortnight for hymn and prayer. This was attended very well, according to the Captain's account, but she implied that many of the people came for aesthetic rather than religious reasons, to hear her solo-singing, and they asked her to sing not the Icelandic hymns but English songs like "Home, sweet home".

The Captain had come out to Iceland with five or six other officers about a year before, but in that time she had learned very little Icelandic. She had a comic way of using Icelandic words in English sentences — "Now I'll deck the board" for "lay the table" — and of expecting to be understood. But perhaps her lack of the language was a good thing, for there was constant friction between herself and the woman who ran the hotel. Kristin was the Captain's Lieutenant, and there were disputes about precedence. Then the Captain thought that she should reprove the false standards of Kristin, who was impressed by people whom she called "fine", for example the dentist and the commercial travellers. I was not considered "fine" because I came to dinner in my breeches though I expect Kristin would have considered me even less fine if I had come without them. On the grounds of the superior standing of the commercial travellers to myself, Kristin wished to turn me out of my balconied bedroom and give it to them, but she found that she was up against a tougher proposition than she imagined, and I stayed in my balcony room. The commercials had to be content with a back one.

But it was a curious weekend for the weather was very hot. There was a sort of sirocco blowing that raised the dust in wreaths and ruffled the waters of the fjord, but it did not dispel the grey mist that brooded over the town. I heard that in some parts this most unusual wind wrecked a seaplane and sank a number of small boats. In Seydisfjord it damaged only the Salvation Army nerves.

The Captain was in a state of excitement the day I arrived, as she and a nice blue-eyed boy who was living in the Hostel thought of walking over to Egilsstadir early on the Sunday morning, staying the night there and returning on Monday. Certainly it was depressing for the poor girl to see the gay crowds hurrying off and to be forced to stay behind. The chief difficulty was her position. As an Army officer she had to be careful of her reputation, and to be seen walking alone with a young man might cause "talk". So I was a heaven-sent chaperon when I arrived at five o'clock in the afternoon, rather tired and muddy. She was all for starting back over the fifteen miles I had just walked. I demurred. Then we should start at four in the morning. I said that I would start not a moment before eight, so we compromised with six. Luckily no one woke before seven, so we were able to get breakfast at a respectable hour and set out about nine. The young man, Sigurbjorn, was wearing white tennis shoes, the Captain had a pair of black high-heeled shoes but went back for white tennis shoes when I suggested she might find walking over the mountains rather exhausting in such flimsy foot-gear. Sigurbjorn carried the lunch in my rucksack and complained at the weight as we toiled up the steep path. We crossed the river with a good deal of giggling and shrieking from the Captain and refusals from us both to be carried across by the handsome Sigurbjorn. I refused because I was too heavy for him and didn't want to be dropped in midstream, she because she was a Captain in the Army and had to set a good example to other girls.

Quite soon it began to rain, so we sheltered under a rock. There we had to restrain Sigurbjorn from eating the lunch as it was not yet eleven. Then the sun came out so we walked a little further. Then it rained again, so we thought we'd better eat the lunch before it got wet. Then Sigurbjorn suggested we should go home, arriving in time for the mid-day lunch. We discussed what they were going to have for lunch down in Seydisfjord, whose distant little roofs we could see from our shelter. But the Captain was quite firm so we went on a little further. Then we rested again. Then we came to a morass. After we had gone three or four miles, the Captain asked how much further it was to Egilsstadir. We told her about twelve miles across the mountain. So she thought it would be better to go home, which we did, getting back in time for afternoon tea, which was lucky as Kristin had just made some fresh pancakes. She was not very pleased to see us. For the rest of the day the Captain and Sigurbjorn sat in my room and played the gramophone. It seemed funny to me that they clung to my chaperonage in this way, as the Captain sleeps in a tiny bedroom that leads off Sigurbjorn's and had to go through his room to reach her own. But to an Icelander, used to the tradition of the *baðstofa* where the men's room communicates with the girls', there is nothing odd in such an arrangement. The Captain told me in a shocked voice how Kristin had behaved when a lot of the English and Icelandic officers were together. They were all (mixed sexes) talking in a large room, which was to be the women's bedroom that night. Kristin got tired and wanted to go to bed, and so she calmly began to undress before the company.

The Captain and I went to the open-air swimming pool, and I had a swim. The water was not warm as the pool was filled from the river which comes down from the mountain swollen with snow-water.

The last day was spent waiting about for the boat. "Esja" was due to arrive at any moment. There was the undercurrent of excitement that runs through these little ports when a boat is expected, hopes of letters and parcels. Several of the men were taking "Esja" back to Akureyri, so we were busy paying our bills, packing and so on. Quite suddenly as we were sitting over the ruins of afternoon coffee, the steamer's whistle blew. We all hurried to fetch our luggage and take the twenty minutes walk to the quay. While we were waiting the Captain introduced me to a fellow-countryman, a fisherman from Hull who had been knocked on the head by a hatchway on his trawler and hurried unconscious to the nearest port. He was enjoying himself and told me how kind the people at the hospital were and how they gave him tea and bread and butter when the other patients were having soup. Then the boat started and I waved goodbye to the two little scraps of jetsam on the quay — the fisherman and the Captain, thrown up on that desolate shore, the one by the rage of the sea, the other by a flood of emotion, to be left high and dry.

The sunset was wonderful. There was a frail moon, and the sky blushed over the sea and snow mountains. The waters of the Heradsfloi, which lay to port, were darker blue than the sea, and the mountains showed like wraiths.

The morning was cloudy, but the sky soon cleared and we sailed in a sea as soft as milk. We stopped at Thorshofn, a desolate little bunch of houses on the edge of a long ridge of shingle. But we couldn't go ashore as the ship did not go in to land. Then we sailed into the Arctic circle. The coast was grim, often low with long shingle stretches. On one of these was the rusty wreck of an English trawler, which had run ashore the previous winter in fog. There was a surprising cliff, Raudinupur,

craggy but set in banks of red earth like Námafjall near
Myvatn. Then we reached Kopasker which is the
shopping town for Grimsstadir and Modrudale. When I
had heard of it on these two farms, I had pictured a gay
metropolis, teeming with traffic, picture theatres and
amusements. There were two or three houses, one of
them the Co-operative warehouse, and a church a mile
or so away.

The sunset was wonderful again, but the colours were
so cold. The mountains facing the sun were a ghostly
grey-blue impossible to describe — not lavender, but
somehow the pale ghost of a lavender that has turned blue
with cold. Then there was a rainbow rising from the
mountain, with straight-up sides — a larger section of
a circle than we commonly feature at home. And there
was Flatey, an insecure little island that seemed to be
floating in the sunset, and looked so low that it might be
submerged in the first high sea. Behind it the sun was
setting in clouds and the sea was shades of pale green, blue-
grey, mauve and pink. It was all very pastel with none
of the stronger shades one sees in the South, or even in
Finland.

Chapter Four

A RIDE IN SKAGAFJORD

THE next morning I was drinking coffee in the Hotel Godafoss in Akureyri. We had turned into Eyjafjord on the previous evening and at last I had been able to return to my dear Godafoss and its comforts. I had a lovely day littering my clothes about my room, fetching letters from the Post Office, eating, bathing and taking gentle walks.

Akureyri seemed a very pretty place to come back to. The street is so gay and the view of the fjord and mountains as lovely as anything in Iceland. I think I should retire there in my old age and snub the English tourists.

I met a great many people I knew there. As I was having lunch on the second day after my return I had a visit from a girl I had met in Reykjavik.[41] She was returning there in a round-about way, and she suggested I should join her in a little detour and do some riding. So we got my heavy luggage packed off to Reykjavik to await my arrival, and I donned once more the riding-kit I had discarded, I thought for good. My friend was going a short motor tour with some friends, and I was to meet her in Skagafjord at a farm called Vidivellir.

I was to go by car on Sunday morning. There were the usual misunderstandings. I was ready for the car and it didn't start; it was ready for me and they couldn't find me. Then it did start and the radiator leaked, the water boiled and the cap flew off on Oxnadalsheidi. The *heiði* was grim and the corners terrifying, taken rather

---

[41] Steinunn Anna Bjarnadóttir (b. 1897). Studied at Westfield College in the University of London 1919–22 and is the author of a text book for English. In 1933 she married Séra Einar Guðnason, the priest at Reykholt in Borgarfjörður which Miss Selby visited on her return journey to Reykjavík (p. 87).

recklessly by our driver who never worried about the ravine below.

I felt rather like Thomas á Becket's mother,[42] as I had two words of information only about our joint plans — Vidivellir and the name of my friend. So when the car stopped and the driver announced that this was Vidivellir, I felt a little unfriended. I walked up to the house and explained in my halting Icelandic that I was the "English girl", and that my friend had told me to meet her there. Happily my hostess seemed to have been forewarned, and I put in two or three hours waiting in the front room. Then my hostess came in with a meal and we talked.

She is a charming and remarkable woman, well known in Iceland for her hospitality.[43] She will not take money for her food and shelter, and as her house lies on the main road between Akureyri and Reykjavik a day never passes without some incursion. She had a tent at the Althing celebrations and for three days served coffee and cakes to any who chose to come. Every year she gives a party to the children of Skagafjord and entertains some hundreds of them. My friend knew her first some years ago, when she was riding in Skagafjord and thrown from her horse. Her wrist was badly hurt, and Lilja took her into the house, nursed her devotedly and would take no payment. Since then she had stayed with my friend in Reykjavik and had invited her to return some time and to bring a friend for a little riding holiday. The invitation had been extended to me, so here I was at Vidivellir.

Lilja is unmarried and so is her twin brother Gisli, who by the curious picaresque convention that I've talked about before turned out to be one of the horse drovers

---

[42] The legendary story of the Saracen maid who came to London seeking Thomas's father can be found in the preface to the *Life of St Thomas* by Edward Grim (Rolls Series, 1876, 455).
[43] Lilja Sigurðardóttir (b. 1884) farmed Víðivellir with her twin brother Gísli for many years. She also taught for a time at the Kvennaskóli in Blönduós.

whom I had met in the East. I felt that the cigarettes that I had unselfishly, and rather reluctantly, as my supply was limited, cast on the water of Jokulsá, were returning to me multiplied tenfold.

Lilja and Gisli then are childless and unmarried, but the house is full of children. There are the children of a sister and two little boys Lilja has adopted. And these boys have friends with them, so there was always a group of blue-dungareed boys in front of the house or leading in the hay, slung in two large bundles, one on each side of a pony's back. Lilja has another comfort — her garden. This is famous in Iceland and many visitors stop to see it. To us with our rich deep soil and the care of centuries, it would seem a pathetic little place, but to the Icelander it is a horticultural wonder. It was blossoming bravely when I saw it with crane's bill and a sort of valerian. There is an attempt at a rockery in the middle, and a few shrubs. Away from the house they've planted some trees, and these are growing as well as they can in the shallow soil and bitter winds.

My friend arrived in the evening with a gay party. They brought with them a most unpleasant medicine which they produced with a good deal of giggling — Icelandic brandy. It was pure alcohol, diluted with water. They laughed and sang, and a nice little clergyman from the next farm led the singing and the gaiety.[44]

It rained all night and the roof leaked, though I had hopefully thought that here at last was a waterproof house. We spent an idle day, eating and hoping the rain would stop. We had two car loads of visitors. The first party was led by a large handsome elderly lady, who smiled a great deal, took her coffee with considered charm, and kissed us all when she left.[45] She is the widow of a well-known poet, and having been a famous

---

[44] Presumably Miklibær. The incumbent at that time was Séra Lárus Arnórsson.
[45] I have been unable to trace the handsome elderly lady.

beauty in her youth has still something of the professional charmer about her. When she had gone, my friend and I went up to our room and read her late husband's poems. We were disturbed by the arrival of a second car which contained the Anglo-American caravan that I had met in the East. I was not altogether surprised to see them as I knew they were coming that way.

When they had gone, we went to the next farm to drink chocolate with the little clergyman of the night before. Then we had supper.

Next day we continued to eat. We had three coffees and a large lunch before we started on our tour at one o'clock. Lilja rode side-saddle and had a long-skirted riding habit. We took a pack-pony, which was a constant nuisance, as it refused to keep up with the other horses and had to be dragged along. So one of us used to ride behind and hit it continually. We followed the motor road and had to go slowly because of the stoney surface. We reached the bridge over the Heradsvatn, the river which provided the delicious trout which was seen dried on the roof of the house. We followed, crossed and re-crossed one of the rivers, and stopped to look at a waterfall and get a distant view of Vidivellir across the Heradsvatn. Lilja told us a pretty story of her old mother.[46] She had lived when she was a child at a farm close by, and in the summer she had often been sent to watch over the sheep near this waterfall. The child, alone in these solitudes, had amused herself by looking across the river to the distant Vidivellir, which was the only house within view. She had sat and dreamed of it through the long summer days, and so closely had the place woven itself into her consciousness that she used to call it "home" and came back to her parents with accounts of what they were doing "at home" that day. Later when she grew up, she met the owner of Vidivellir, married him and so it became in reality her home.

[46] Guðrún Pétursdóttir, born at Reykir in Tungusveit in 1852.

We left the waterfall and climbed a stoney track, and seemed to be penetrating uninhabited regions — mountains, stones, an occasional pony, but no house. It was nine o'clock and was getting dark. Still we rode and still there were no houses. At last, at ten o'clock, we saw a grey house through the dusk — a fine stone house with large windows and a long flight of steps. This was Tunguháls, where we intended to spend the night. Lilja went up to the front door and knocked gently, but there was no sign of life. Then she tried the door and peered in. Anna joined her and I was left alone with the horses. They disappeared into the house and came back to say that no one was stirring. There was a sort of assembly hall where we might be able to sleep, but the prospect was cheerless as we hadn't eaten since one o'clock. They went off to investigate the hay house, thinking that it might be warmer than the bare boards of the assembly hall. Then through the dusk I saw the door of the grey house open and a skirt or something fluttered round the edge. It looked rather uncanny in the half-light, and wearied by the long ride I wondered if here perhaps was a house of the dead and that one of them had risen and the grave clothes were fluttering in the wind. Anna and Lilja were still hidden behind the hay house. After a few seconds the door opened a little more and the ghost came out — a young woman who had obviously put on a dress over her nightgown, hence the fluttering effect.

The evening was still ghost-like. We unsaddled the horses in the dark and went into the dark house, where we sat in a large hall and could but faintly perceive two large ornamental windows, a great litter of bedclothes, and some books. We talked together in whispers, and the ghost woman hurried about with mattresses and bedding. Then we were led through a long room full of sleeping men and women. There were two beds on each side of the room, and in one of them a child coughed

uneasily in its sleep. We came into a little room and
dimly saw two nice white beds. Then we had a meal
taken blindly, but my sense of taste told me that it was
rye bread and butter with milk, and finally fumbling
with our clothes in the dark fell at last into bed.

Next morning the sun shone, and after a meal we started
up Vesturdale. We crossed the bridge over Jokulsá
and made for Hofsdale. After riding for perhaps two
hours we came upon the farmer from Gil, a house at which
we had called on our way up the valley. Our tour was
in a sense a social one, at least for Lilja, and she had a
great many calls to make at different farms. The farmer
from Gil was at his hay-making on a little estate with a
deserted farmhouse that he had rented.[47] While Lilja and
he chatted, I sat and dreamed that I should take the
deserted farmhouse and live in this solitary dale for the
rest of my life. I had just reached the point of furnishing
the *eldhús* when the farmer said we must go down to the
river and see the view. It was very fine, as the river
flows through a deep ravine. We climbed about on the
crags and looked at the little flowers growing in the
cracks of the cliff. Then there was a great discussion
as to whether we should go further up the valley. The
farmer was enthusiastic that we should and offered to
accompany us. Another two or three hours ride up the
dale would give us a splendid view of the glaciers of central
Iceland. In the end the project was reluctantly
abandoned; it was now four o'clock and we had five
or six hours ride to reach the farm where we intended
to spend the night. I was interested to see the
recklessness and hardihood of the Icelandic character in
this discussion. Lilja was particularly eager to see the
glaciers and was prepared to forego food and sleep to
do so. We had no food with us, and as far as I could see
no chance of getting any as the upper part of the dale
was uninhabited. We had had nothing since we left

[47] Probably Þorljótsstaðir in Vesturdalur.

Tunguháls at ten that morning. When we discussed the
question of sleep, they said airily, "We shall just have to
lie down in the open for a few hours." Later I discussed
this question of hardihood with Anna and she admitted
that it was an important quality in the Icelandic
character today as it had been with the saga-folk of old.
It is closely linked with their pride; she says that the
motor-drivers on the road from Reykjavik to Akureyri
are prepared to drive eighteen hours without rest, and
this on a road that taxes both muscle and nerve as the
surface and the gradients are very trying.

But I think that my two friends were influenced on this
occasion by consideration for the English lack of hardihood; with many backward glances at the invisible
glaciers we turned our horses' heads in the direction of
Mælifell where we hoped to stay the night. It was a
good thing perhaps that we did turn back. We had
several minor mishaps. I got my boots full of water as
we crossed the river. Lilja was sick because we drank
some sour cream at a farm. Then her horse came down
on some loose stones, and she fell. Fortunately she was
not hurt, but the frightened horses had to be pacified.
It seemed a long way to Mælifell and we didn't get there
before ten-thirty. The sunset was beautiful, the sky very
pink in the east and the mountains grey and blue. We
filed through the magic twilight, a very tired caravan,
Lilja at the head, bravely perched on her pillion saddle,
Anna leading the pack-pony, and me at the rear occasionally flicking at the animal in a half-hearted way. But,
curiously, when we reached Mælifell in a state of the
utmost exhaustion and fell stiffly off our horses, the
exhaustion vanished. We found the house still awake,
as they were awaiting the return of the clergyman. We
had a blind supper, smoked salmon on bread — I think.

Then Anna and I went to bed and talked so long that
I thought the household would protest. We discussed
the quality of *hǫfðingskapr* (liberality, or to translate

the word literally, the disposition of a chieftain). We thought that Lilja, and her brother, and her mother had it. It seemed odd to use the word of the mother — a gentle, dirty old woman, who sits on the front steps with her knitting on summer evenings. But it was quite true that the courtesy and consideration with which she treated her tiresome and rather inarticulate English visitor might well deserve the term. And the hospitality that they delight to show — they invited eighty members of a glee-club to a party — is like the lavishness and liberality of a chieftain of old.

The next day was very hot, and everyone exclaimed at the heat. It seemed a nice warm summer day to me. We were going to climb a mountain near the house and get, perhaps, a view of the jokuls we missed the day before. But as everyone was sitting about groaning at the heat, it was decided to give up the idea. We sat about and drank several coffees. Some other visitors drifted in, so we had some more coffee. My friend and I were to ride to some point on the main Akureyri and Reykjavik road and intercept a car which would take us to Blonduós. There we were to spend the night, and I was to travel on to Reykjavik the next day with the same car. Anna was to stay in Blonduós with friends.

We started in the early afternoon, and it was pleasant riding in the warm sun, though the horses seemed disinclined to hurry. So we dawdled along with frequent rests. I was getting a little anxious, as the car which we were to intercept was scheduled to leave Saudárkrokur at four. But I consoled myself by the thought that the driver had no better time-sense than other Icelanders I had met. It was well after four when we came in sight of the main road, and almost immediately we saw a car drive past. The thought that it was ours made us urge the horses to a gallop. So followed a comic cinema chase. The car was proceeding fairly fast along a long flat road, it turned uphill where the road began to zigzag up a mountain side. We shouted and hallooed, but the car ignored us. We flogged our horses, and they simulated a gallop which was in reality no faster than a trot. In fact we provided an excellent slow-motion picture where all the movements of the gallop are produced but the pace is of the snail. We hooted and clattered for about two miles after the fast receding car, and the dust flew from under our horses' hoofs. Finally we reached a farm and a petrol pump, and gave up the chase. We enquired from the man at the farm who told us that we had been chasing an illusion, for the car was not driven by Páll but contained some quite irrelevant tourists from Akureyri. To add to the comedy, the car now came back slowly along the road for its occupants had decided to fill up with petrol before climbing the pass over the mountains.

It was nice to rest here at Vidimyri, to cool ourselves and to inspect the old church;[48] there is some pretty woodwork inside, including high carved pew-ends and some old painted inscriptions.

Then a car arrived, driven not by Páll but by the young man who had brought me from Svarfadardale that wet Sunday, which now seemed so long ago. As we didn't know whether Páll was ahead or behind, we decided to travel in this car. So we said goodbye to Lilja who was riding back to Vidivellir with the horses, and we turned up over the *heiði*. We had a lovely ride, and the view from the top was superb as we could see Langjokull and Hofsjokull. We ought also to have been able to look down Skagafjord to the sea, but at that point the *þoka* descended. We came down into Langidale and saw where the Svartá (the Black river, which is transparent) met Blanda (the mixed river that is opaque, formed from the melting glacier snows). My friend told me how the snow-rivers vary in height from hour to hour and how in

---

[48] The old turf church at Víðimýri was built in 1834–5 by Einar Stefánsson, the grandfather of the poet Einar Benediktsson.

the morning many of the rivers are quite safe to cross, whilst in the evenings, particularly after a warm day, they are swollen by the melting snows and extremely dangerous to cross. Langidale was very pretty in the afternoon sun. It is a wide, peaceful valley and the mountains are not too high or terrifying. Men and women were hay-making in the flat meadows by the river.

Then we drove out of the sun into *þoka*, and the descent into Blonduós was like passing from summer into winter. The place seems horrid, little low houses creeping round a grey sea which was dashing against the pebbles of the beach. The sea birds were screaming. It is surprising to find how the weather varies within a small area in Iceland. One dale may be enjoying the sun, the next is in mist or actual rain. I was told that the weather in Akureyri was never the same as that in Reykjavik. So that sun in Akureyri always means rain in Reykjavik.

I found it curious coming back to responsibilities and organisation again. The last few days I had been so well looked after by my friends that I had felt as if I was on a Cook's tour. I had gone where I was taken, eaten my meals when I was told — usually at most unusual hours, and I had slept when the others slept. Now I was Master of my Fate again. I had looked forward to an hotel in Blonduós. Indeed there was one, but it was untidy and uncomfortable, and the supper was not punctual. Indeed I found in most of the hotels I stayed in or ate in that the standard of comfort was much lower than in private houses. Possibly this is one of the many manifestations of Icelandic pride. If you are accepting hospitality as a guest (even if he knows you will pay a small sum when you leave), he does his best to make you comfortable, feeling probably that he is your host. But when the element of commercialism comes in and you are buying food and lodging from him, he does not feel bound to study your comfort. Further, pride forbids the Icelandic guest to complain, even if the hotel is uncomfortable and the food poor and tardy. In this hotel I was woken up in the middle of the night by an unexpected guest who was parked in my bedroom. The guest rose at five-thirty and did her toilet with just enough noise to wake me, and just enough hush to be irritating.

Chapter Five

RETURN TO REYKJAVIK AND FAREWELL

I FELT rather cross when we did start, as we hurried over our breakfast to be ready by seven, the scheduled time, and then waited half an hour for the apothecary and his wife, who had overslept.[49] The apothecary's wife was soon *bílveik*. The road twisted along the course of an old pony track, and the swaying motion evidently upset the lady. But I think the horrors of motoring in Iceland are much exaggerated. We were fourteen hours on the way, and nearly all of it was agreeable and very little of it terrifying. I believe that in wet weather it is much worse. All the cars carry a spade or two with which the car can be dug out of the mud if it sinks too deeply.

The most striking feature of the landscape in the earlier part of the ride was a curious formation of little hills at the mouth of Vatnsdale. Here are countless little mounds (and I use the word countless as more than a cliché, for I was told that there was a superstition that no one could count these hills twice and get the same total). They looked like children's sand mounds poured from a bucket or, even more prosaically, like a very large collection of rubbish dumps.

We stopped at Grænumyrartunga for coffee before crossing the long long *heiði*, which was so incredibly boring that I fell asleep. When I awoke we were following a river and descended into a flood of *hraun* in a district of low scrub. We passed several hot springs and arrived at Reykholt, formerly the home of Snorri Sturluson, at three in the afternoon. Nowadays there is a grand new

---

[49] Helgi apótekari, as he was called, was Þorvarðarson. He worked as a pharmacist for his brother-in-law Kristján Arinbjarnar who was the doctor in Blönduós at the time. Helgi's wife's name was Jakobína.

building there — in winter a school and in summer a hotel. It is centrally heated from the hot springs, and I greatly enjoyed washing my hands in a nice white basin with new taps. We had a meal there. My fellow passengers sat down at three-thirty on a hot afternoon to stewed mutton followed by porridge. I noticed that none of them complained at the unsuitability of the fare. I should have done, but had anticipated by insisting on some cold food. We climbed up onto Kaldadalsheidi and had a marvellous view of the glaciers — Langjokul and Eiriksjokul — and the bleakest expanse of country — stones, mud, snow, not a blade of grass, and the road zigzagging across the grey and stoney surface. Here no road-makers have been at work, the cars have simply cut a track across the soft rubble of the mountains.

Then there were more mountains, some of them looking very insecure and with rocks that seemed to be shifting as we passed. We saw Skjaldbreid, a tame affair, I thought, to have made all the mess of lava that became Thingvellir. Then a narrow pass between two mountains of rubble and we came down under the ridge that runs on to form Almannagjá. Now there was a nice quick ride along what seemed a marvellously smooth road. I had to remind myself with some effort of the time I jolted along this same road when I first visited Thingvellir, and I reflected how one's standards change. Soon we were in Reykjavik and it all seemed urban and over-populated.

I found my luggage waiting for me at the Hotel Island.[50] I was pleased to unpack the things I felt I had lost some years before. I went down to the restaurant and had a meal of asparagus soup and fruit salad — the items on the menu that most forcibly symbolised civilization and cosmopolitanism to me at the moment. The place seemed brilliantly lighted, and the third-rate dancing and music incredibly gay. I gaped for some time like a hay-seed, went out into the streets and looked in a daze at the

---

[50] The Hotel Ísland was in the main street and burned down in 1944.

lighted shop windows and teaming crowds of passers-by. Then I went to bed.

Breakfast next morning presented a bewildering variety of fancy and plain breads. I had a bath, dressed in leisure, went to fetch my letters, had my hair cut, met a great many people that I knew, and received an invitation to a child's birthday party.

The party seemed to me a very sensible one. The child was ill in bed, so the grown-ups gorged chocolate, whipped-cream cakes and coffee, while the child was allowed a scrap of cake and a sip of chocolate. The family, which is a huge one, talked English and we were very gay.

At this party was a pretty girl, the fiancée of one of the young men. She was a pretty fragile thing with a pale face, broad brow and large greenish eyes set far apart. I noticed that she was smiling and bowing from time to time in an unmotivated way. When I had left I mentioned this to my friends. They replied, "Oh, she was only greeting the dead relations as they came into the room to join the party." Further, they told me that if this girl came to see them she would often look round rather vaguely after entering the room. "Won't you sit down," her hostess would say. "I'm sorry, I can't," she would reply. "All the chairs are occupied." And this in a room where the hostess was sitting alone waiting for her guests. We met the same girl the next morning. "I'm so tired this morning," she said. "A friend," and she mentioned the name of a girl who had died a day or two ago, "came to see me last night and she stayed talking so long that I had to turn on the light to get rid of her."

I went to see the Einar Jonsson sculptures which are housed in a new and modernistic building. I had heard a great deal of this sculptor for the Icelanders are very proud of him. Iceland is in a sense a paradise for artists and poets. The intense national pride creates a sympathetic feeling towards any form of art displayed by a fellow-countryman. The government creates nice soft jobs for the poets, librarianships and the like, so that the artist can live untroubled by the struggle for existence and produce his masterpieces at leisure. It is surprising to observe the feeling that most of the people have about poetry, particularly if the verse is of a geographical nature and is written about waterfalls and mountains. Poetry with this theme is far more popular and also more emotional than love poetry. Often I noticed that the people I met would quote some poem at an appropriate spot — as if a member of a charabanc party in England should talk about "this precious stone, set in a silver sea" when he had the first glimpse of the Channel from the South Downs. Even tiny children would lisp the more famous of the national songs. I think it is part of the same feeling that created the sagas, an intense nationalism and a love of their country and of the particular corner of it they know, so that the events and people of that district become of the utmost importance in the minds of the poet or saga-writer. In the poetry, however, the concern is mainly with natural objects and is not projected into the inhabitants of a district, so that to me personally there is a bleakness in the verse. I can't keep on being interested in a waterfall as I can in a person.

I found Einar Jonsson's sculpture disappointing. His best work is that in which there is a design, where he is building round a pattern, triangle or cross. The Mountain Troll is rather impressive, a woman who is saved from the troll by the rays of the rising sun. His later work is spoiled by a detailed symbolism, which often seems to me to be merely funny. There is a statue of Evolution — a horse, out of which grows an ape, then a man, then a cross and a small figure praying. His naturalistic work did not convince me. His female figures though striving to imitate the human form have a curious lack of force.

I tried bathing in Reykjavik, but it was not a great

success. The water was exceedingly cold, the sunshine in which we sat after bathing was tempered, and the foreshore dirty and strewn with miscellaneous objects.

That evening I went with a friend for a picnic and walk across the lava to Hafnarfjord. We took a car out to the Sanatorium and walked from there.[51] It was a lovely evening and the sun put all sorts of magic colours on the sea, the mountains and the lava. We sat and chattered in the twilight till it grew so dark that we could hardly find our way across the jagged lava rocks. It was night by the time we arrived in Hafnarfjord. The little town by the sea seemed very romantic with its small houses and their lighted windows. Late as it was, my friend took me back to her home, and I saw her mother, a wonderful old lady, whose photograph has been incorporated in a German collection of Women of All Nations.[52] The old lady is like a woman of the sagas and will keep the control of her household in her wrinkled hands to the very last. Suitably enough she is a sort of curator in the Museum of Antiquities, and in her the visitor will see a much more potent reminder of the days of old than in the woven and embroidered fabrics that moulder in the glass cases with a scent of moth ball.

I went the next day to see the Museum. The old ladies who guard it would be very little protection against burglars. I was amused at this ingenious method of the Icelandic government of pensioning off its distinguished but impecunious old ladies. I called at the Natural History Museum, but did not find the birds and fish interesting enough to drown the natural atmosphere of death and corruption.

I had puffin for lunch next day, an agreeable bird not unlike goose in flavour. Then I made an expedition to

---

[51] Vífilsstaðir, a tuberculosis sanatorium.
[52] I have been unable to trace the German book, but "the old lady" was almost certainly Guðríður Guðmundsdóttir, the wife of Matthías Þórðarson, the curator of the Museum of Antiquities. The daughter's name was Sigríður.

Hafnarfjord, which I had already seen in the romantic darkness of the night before. The place was less interesting in the clear light of the early afternoon, but there is a little garden in the lava which is appealing if only for the human optimism to which it bore witness.[53]

That night I left Reykjavik in the "Gullfoss". I had left undone many of the things I had meant to do. I had no time to visit Hekla and the Geysirs, to see the waterfall Gullfoss, and — the thing I regret most — to visit Hlidarendi, where the brave Gunnarr of *Njálssaga* lost his life.

It was dark when the boat left. There were faint reflections of the sunset, and I amused myself by pretending that I was seeing the Northern Lights, though I knew it was too early in the year for this phenomenon. I was touched, as we moved slowly off, to look down on the crowd of up-turned faces and shadowy forms on the quay.

We had a long wait at Vik on the south coast while countless sacks of wool were brought on board. The shore is too exposed here and the sea too rough to allow of motor boats, so the sacks of wool were piled in large eight-oared boats. It was amusing to see these boats being launched. They were carried to the water's edge on the shoulders of a great many men, so they looked like beetles or centipedes — a rounded shell above a series of trotting legs.

My last parting from things Icelandic was sad. We had a cargo of ponies, poor little things packed tightly, head to tail in pens of eight, in the hold. They are packed so tightly to prevent them lying down and so being trodden on.

I left the boat at Leith as they were being unloaded, each one strapped onto a pulley and suspended in the air before it was gently lowered to the quay. It was sad to

---

[53] This small park is known as Hellisgerði.

think that they were destined to the eternal darkness of the pit — gallant little Icelanders who had cropped the sweet grass and frisked in the sunshine of their native mountain-sides.

ALICE SELBY

A personal recollection by G. R. Hibbard

I STILL remember my first meeting with Alice. It was the beginning of the Autumn Term in 1934; and I was one of a class about to make its first acquaintance with the History of the English Language and the mysteries of Indo-European Philology. Alice came in, sun-tanned, vigorous, alert, and began to teach. There was no introductory waffle. She had a job to do, she knew how to do it, and she got on with it. By the end of the hour it was already abundantly plain to us that at least one philologist was emphatically not the dry-as-dust pedant that the study of philology was popularly supposed to produce. We had felt the impress not only of superb teaching but also of a highly individual personality.

At that time Alice was Senior Lecturer in English in the University College, as it then was, of Nottingham, which, having no charter of its own, prepared its students for the External Examinations of the University of London. She had been there for sixteen years, having joined the staff of the English Department in 1918, after completing her studies at Cambridge. It was a tiny department, tucked away in a provincial backwater, but it was vital, creative, and exciting in a manner that makes many of the large English departments in our universities today look lethargic and elephantine. All the essential work was done by three people: and what remarkable people they were! Utterly unlike each other in almost every respect, they formed a perfect team. Poet, polyglot, and enthusiast for learning, the Head of the Department, Reginald Mainwaring Hewitt, with a lock of white hair sweeping over his high-domed forehead, seemed like a reincarnation of the Renaissance ideal of the man who took all knowledge for his province. Blessed with a prodigious memory, he imparted information, much of it rare and out of the way, with unstinting generosity and unfaltering eloquence. George Stuart Griffiths, on the other hand, was a man of intuitive insights. He would often begin a lecture in what appeared to be a rather fumbling manner as he searched for the right opening into his subject, but, having found that opening, he caught fire, as it were, and said things that many of his students have never forgotten. Alice's special contribution, particularly in all matters that affected the day to day running of the Department, was that rare commodity, good, hard common sense. Overworked — Alice, for example, taught Anglo-Saxon, Middle English, and Old Norse in addition to the History of the Language — and underpaid, eking out their salaries by doing extra-mural teaching in the evenings, they had neither the time nor the opportunity to engage on any scale in the publication by which the academic world of today sets such store, even had they wished to do so. In fact, they did not. Highly civilised and very much alive to the nature of the world they were living in, they regarded the competitive spirit which prompts so much "research" with a proper degree of suspicion. They wrote only when they felt they had something to say; and the standards by which they decided whether a thing was worth saying or not were extremely high. But they never neglected their students. Far from being "unproductive", they helped to produce what a university should produce: men and women capable of making the most of such intellectual endowments as they have.

In 1935 I began to read Old Norse with Alice, and continued to do so until I left Nottingham in 1938. It was a richly rewarding experience, for, of all the subjects she taught, this was the closest to her heart. At the centre of her interest in the past, and in the present too for that matter, was her feeling for everyday life.

She never allowed us to forget that philology was about the speech habits of men who had lived and laboured on this earth; that *Beowulf* came out of a specific kind of society, with its own organization and its own rules. The sagas ministered, to an extent that no other older literature could, to her love of the factual and to her instinctive response to the hard realities of life. But her absorption in them also revealed another side of her nature to me, which I had barely glimpsed until then: practical, competent, efficient though she was, she also had something of the romantic in her. She delighted in the extreme individualism of the saga heroes; their adventurous journeys struck an answering chord in her; and she admired the ethos that prompted their last stands. The journey she had recently made to Iceland had evidently not been without its sentimental — in the very best sense of that word — motives and overtones.

For a period, during the early years of the Second World War, Alice was in charge of the English Department at Nottingham; but from 1939 until 1946 I was out of touch with her. In the Spring Term of 1946, after being demobilized, I returned to Nottingham as a lecturer, and for the next five years we were colleagues, until she finally retired from university teaching in 1951, after working on a part-time basis for several years. Characteristically, Alice's retirement was no ordinary retirement. Active by nature and of an enterprising temperament, she had no intention of sitting down to do nothing in particular. Instead, she had decided to embark on a new way of life which would also be an assertion of her attachment to traditional ways. Knowing that acceptance by a rural community is a slow and difficult process, she had taken the first steps towards a change of occupation in the mid-thirties, when she bought a cottage in the village of Kniveton, near Ashbourne. There she spent her week-ends and vacations, immersing herself in village life. Then, in 1944, she bought Church Farm,

in the same village, and, with the help of her sister
Dorothea, adventurously set about running it, applying
her ability to learn to the acquisition of new skills and
also new items of vocabulary. By this time she was not
only well known to the villagers but had also won their
respect and trust, with the result that she became their
representative on the Rural District Council, where she
was able to put her good sense about matters in general,
together with her specialized knowledge of education, to
practical use in the service of the community to which
she now belonged. She eventually gave up the farm in
1953, to move into a house she had built on the other side
of the little Anglo-Saxon church, but she continued to
participate in the life of the village.

In 1946 my debt to Alice was deep. In the years that
followed it became immeasurably deeper. Visiting her,
first at the farm and then at the Croft, was one of life's
major pleasures. Good conversation was assured. At
times it turned on village happenings, in which she took
the keenest interest, often making them into minor sagas.
More frequently it touched on larger topics and issues:
history, politics, religion, the emancipation of women, to
which her own life was a testimony, and so forth. To her
discussion of them she brought that profound respect
for facts and that sceptical attitude towards opinions
which had been the very basis of her teaching. She never
hesitated to say exactly what she thought, and what she
thought was always worth thinking about. To know her
was a liberal education. To know her well, in all her
freshness of mind and generosity of spirit, was to feel a
strong and abiding affection for her. She belonged
to no school, she followed no fashion, she was her own
unique self.